Knowledge and Relativism

D1459712

KNOWLEDGE AND RELATIVISM

An Essay in the Philosophy of Education

by F.C. White

Department of Philosophy,
University of Tasmania, Australia

1983
Van Gorcum, Assen, The Netherlands

CIP-gegevens

White, F.C.

Knowledge and relativism: an essay in the philosophy of education / by F.C. White. - Assen: Van Gorcum
Met index, lit. opg.
SISO 100   UDC 1
Trefw.: filosofie
ISBN 90 232 1932 5

Printed in The Netherlands by Van Gorcum, Assen

To Caroline and Stewart

CONTENTS

ACKNOWLEDGMENTS

I am grateful to my colleagues in the department for their many helpful comments, to Mrs. N. Gill for her typing, to Dr. W. Nesbitt, Mr. P. Simpson and to my wife for proof-reading, and to the editors of *Educational Philosophy & Theory* for allowing me to make extensive use of material which appeared in their journal.

F.C. White

INTRODUCTION

Among the many questions looked at by philosophers concerned with education, the following two stand out as being of more than average importance. What should children do while they are at school? Is the learning or
knowledge which children acquire at school, from morals to science, any
more than relative to their teachers' culture, sub-culture or even social class?

The former question is important in two ways. First, it concerns what *ends*
should be achieved at school; and until that issue has been settled there
would seem to be little point in going on to others. Discussions over such
things as when, how and in what conditions learning should take place are
plainly parasitic upon what in the first place is to be done at all. Second, this
question is one over which, despite the repeated efforts of philosophers, there
is still great disagreement and uncertainty. The discussion needs to be continued.

The second question is important because what may with reasonable
plausibility be termed the traditional view of education assumes not only that
knowledge has some worth in itself (as well as in its consequences), but that it
possesses *objectivity*, and this latter assumption has satisfied most generations
so far that teachers do more than impose upon their pupils beliefs which are
of passing value, the prejudices of this or that culture, sub-culture or class.
Under two separate theses, however, this traditional view has recently been
severely challenged.

The first of these theses is a philosophical one, consisting principally in a
criticism of the rationalist and the earlier empiricist views of knowledge.
According to these views, men have available to them (to their reason or to
their senses) a number of given, basic and incontrovertible pieces of knowledge, upon which they are able subsequently to build and develop an equally
solid superstructure. But, this first thesis argues, there are strong reasons for
saying that there simply are no such unshakeable foundations to knowledge;
that instead our beliefs are all provisional, embedded in a framework which
is open to piecemeal alteration, adjustment and innovation.

The second thesis is partly philosophical, partly sociological, and its
principal tenet is that all men's beliefs are the products of the societies,
cultures or sub-cultures of which they form part. That is, all beliefs are
socially or culturally determined, and therefore have no legitimacy beyond

1

the societies or cultures which have given them birth. In a word, truth itself is socially and culturally relative.

This doctrine of cultural relativism has become, in one form or another, so much part of our general climate of opinion, that students of education, philosophy and sociology tend to take it for granted. But when it comes to saying precisely what doctrine of cultural relativism this or that sociologist, philosopher or educationist subscribes to, there are often great difficulties. For, to begin with, the expression 'cultural relativism' itself is employed by different writers in different and conflicting ways.[1] Secondly, sociologists — partly under the influence of a German tradition — often attach meanings of their own to such centrally important terms as 'knowledge' and 'reality',[2] and for this reason tend to be at cross purposes in discussion with others. Thirdly, not a few writers in the field have a style and turn of phrase which is more than usually obscure.[3] Finally, strong feelings and commitment on one side or other sometimes give rise to a rhetoric which at best conceals and at worst takes the place of analysis and argument.[4] Perhaps it would be fair to add that the question of relativism is one of considerable intrinsic difficulty anyway.

Nonetheless, despite the difficulties and obscurities, there is little doubt that the doctrine of cultural relativism in various forms has been and still is widely and professionally espoused. A start in bringing this out may be made with a quotation from D. Gorbutt, concerning P. Berger and T. Luckmann's much acclaimed book, *The Social Structure of Reality*. 'Knowledge at all levels, common sense, theoretical and scientific, thereby becomes thoroughly relativised and the possibility of absolute knowledge is denied. Whereas Marx and Mannheim, key figures in the sociology of knowledge, asserted that some knowledge can be free from social bias, Berger and Luckmann argue that all knowledge is socially constructed and ideological. Truth and objectivity are human products.'[5] In a similar vein, M. Young, in his widely discussed collection, *Knowledge and Control*, apparently argues that there can be no common ('objective') way of establishing what counts as knowledge, since what counts as knowledge is determined by teachers, and is relative to the position of the latter in society. More generally, he argues, all knowledge is socially constructed, subject to change and relative to the cultures of those who possess it.[6] In the same collection, A. Blum argues that knowledge is the product of particular groups ('intellectual collectivities'), and that 'it is not an objectively discernible purely existing external world which accounts for sociology; it is the methods and procedures of sociology which create and sustain that world'.[7]

Arguments and claims of this kind are used by writers of the 'school' of Young, Esland and others, to defend the view that since knowledge (as they claim) is socially constructed, neither teachers nor others have the right to impose a *common* system of knowledge on children and students. Moreover, since many of those writing in this manner are Marxists or Neo-Marxists

2

anyway, they hold that, at any rate in liberal democracies, 'children do not simply learn maths, English, history and so on; they learn what certain ruling interests take as maths, English and history; and they accept as correct and worth knowing what those same interests count as correct and worth knowing'.[8] They hold further that 'ruling groups, through their power on committees, their control over journals and publication in general and their "positions", determine what shall pass as mathematics, history, geography, science, philosophy etc., in any particular epoch'.[9]

Behind views of this kind, expressed by those who are explicitly concerned with the problems of education, there is a wider background of sociological and philosophical thought which to some extent their proponents are justified in turning to. It was the teaching of Marx, for example, that the dominant view of knowledge in a society at a given epoch is that of the currently ruling class. Rather similarly, Mannheim held that, with the exception of mathematics and the natural sciences, even the content of men's beliefs is determined by class: that people of different classes perceive reality in different ways, and that only the socially unattached intelligentsia is in a position to be free from bias. More recently, D. Bloor has tried to show that Mannheim was wrong to make an exception of mathematics or anything else,[10] and Berger and Luckmann are interpreted as having attempted much the same: as holding that in some non-trivial sense all knowledge as well as reality is socially constructed.[11] Sociologists on occasion even speak with open praise of the (extreme) relativism of Protagoras and his fellow sophists.[12]

In philosophy too there is more than one recent strand which might with justification be looked to by the relativist. The later Wittgenstein,[13] for example, can reasonably be taken to have advanced a doctrine of thoroughgoing relativism, and so may such of his followers as P. Winch and D.Z. Phillips (despite disclaimers).[14] In a different tradition, Quine — particularly the early Quine[15] — may be held to have done much the same. In yet a further (Collingwoodian) tradition, S. Körner has attempted in a more systematic and explicit manner to defend the relativity of the foundations of science, logic and metaphysics,[16] and several others have from time to time undertaken at least part of such a task by defending a (non-trivial) doctrine of the conventional status of logic.[17] Finally, much that has been written recently on the philosophy of science by Kuhn, Lakatos, Feyerabend and others may fairly be interpreted as having strongly relativistic implications.[18]

To return for a moment to M. Young and his colleagues. In his recent book, *Illusions of Equality*,[19] David Cooper has given a considerable amount of space to examining their claims, and his discussion of them is exemplary. He concedes that there is no possibility of making coherent sense of their philosophical views, and what he does instead is to outline what he considers the most plausible position which they might be *interpreted* as holding. With this end in view and with the licence of considerable generosity, he treats

3

their subjectivist remarks as expressions of the 'pragmatist' doctrines of philosophers like Popper and Quine;[20] their remarks on unity of knowledge (against subject-divisions and so on) as following recent and respectable views (stemming from Quine and others) on the distinction between *a priori* and *a posteriori* knowledge; and their relativistic remarks as in part following from their subjectivist views and in part concerned with those quite special cases where alternative logics have application. He then goes on to argue that even on these plausible interpretations Young and his followers are not entitled to draw the educational conclusions which they so passionately urge. For, as he patiently points out, these philosophical doctrines imply nothing against such things as the existence of expertise and authority among teachers, nothing against the divisions into subjects which tradition has handed down to us, and nothing which might countenance such views as that 'anything goes' in mathematics or whatever other subject.

I think that Cooper is to be admired for what he accomplishes here, since if anything urgently needs to be done at the moment, it is to pin down and shed light on many of the positions and arguments of radical educationists which so far have only been hinted at, or at best sketched out in a way which leaves them open to conflicting interpretations. One way to do this is Cooper's way:[21] to construct a favourable and plausible interpretation of what is obscurely and perhaps inconsistently said, and then to examine the implications of the resulting doctrine. My own approach, while in the same spirit and concerned with the same problem, is rather different. I attempt to bring out as clearly and systematically as possible what Young and others, whatever their words or intentions, could *not* plausibly have held on the nature of knowledge and its relation to society.

The plan of the book is as follows. Chapter 1 examines the extremest of all forms of the doctrine of social or cultural relativism: that form according to which men can make no claims to knowledge of any kind which are not relative to their respective societies or cultures. It also draws attention, though in passing, to another extreme but contrasting thesis of relativism: that which concerns itself not with specific cultures but with human nature in general, or perhaps with the nature of all sentient and intelligent beings. This thesis is returned to in Chapter 7.

Chapter 2 starts upon the examination of the major areas of knowledge, or candidates for knowledge, and looks at the status of claims made in the natural sciences, while Chapter 3 continues with a parallel look at the claims of the social sciences. In both cases it is argued that the doctrine of cultural relativism is far from satisfactory.

Chapters 4 and 5 focus on the problem of moral claims, arguing that the latter are not, at any rate all, culturally relative. A large amount of space is given to this discussion, since not only is the problem of the status of moral claims arguably more important than others concerned with the curriculum, but because the central thesis of these chapters hinges on an analysis of what

4

it means to make rational choices, and the outcome of that analysis lays the foundation for the treatment of the curriculum in general.

Chapter 6 finally takes up the question of what children should do in school, arguing that a curriculum can be arrived at through rational discussion, and that what should go into it is therefore not a matter merely of what this or that social group or culture chooses.

Chapter 7, as was mentioned, returns to the wider issue of relativism, attempting to show that while the doctrine of cultural relativism is plainly untenable, the same cannot fairly be said of its transcultural pair. The latter however, it will be argued, has no bearing on the problem of education.

CHAPTER 1
TOTAL CULTURAL RELATIVISM

This first chapter concerns what will be referred to as the doctrine of total cultural relativism, and to bring out what is meant by this it will be useful to distinguish on the one hand between cultural and transcultural relativism, and on the other hand between partial and total cultural relativism.

Cultural, by contrast with transcultural relativism, is the doctrine that the truth of men's beliefs is relative to and determined by the sub-groups to which severally they belong: to nation, class, religion, civilisation or whatever. Transcultural relativism is the doctrine that men's apprehension or awareness of reality is not relative, or not relative merely, to this or that particular sub-group or culture, but to mankind as a whole, or perhaps to all intelligent and sentient beings. Partial cultural relativism is the fairly modest claim that some, but only some, of men's beliefs are culturally determined and therefore culturally relative; total cultural relativism is the bolder and more sweeping claim that all are.

The nature of relative beliefs

In order to establish that any given set of beliefs is relative, three things need first to be shown. One, that there exists, or may exist, an alternative set of beliefs which is different from and not complementary to the initial set. Two, that we have no means of deciding rationally which set is correct, or that neither is correct. Three, that it does not even make sense to say that this or that set is correct to the exclusion of the other; or again that neither is correct.[1]

It is important to bear in mind that the fulfilment of the second of these requirements does not entail the fulfilment of the third. That is, if we have no means of deciding which beliefs are correct or incorrect, it does not of itself follow that there is no sense to saying that one set, and only one set, is correct, or that both are incorrect. Examples will illustrate this. We might have no means of deciding whether or not Henry II commanded the murder of Thomas Becket, but without doubt it makes sense to say that only one of these alternatives was realised: that either he did or did not issue the command. Similarly, we might not have the means of deciding whether the same Henry spent the Christmas of 1185 at Rouen or Woodstock, or at neither; but clearly it makes sense to say that one and only one of the three possibilities was fulfilled.

The purpose of underlining this is to insist that if any kind of relativist argument is to succeed, independent support must first be provided for its 'no sense' claims. In particular cases independent arguments are of course quite frequently provided. For example, it is convincingly argued that when people have conflicting beliefs concerning which is the proper side of the road to drive on, it makes no sense to say that one party is correct and the other not. It makes no sense precisely because we can show that which side of the road is to be driven on is a matter of explicit convention. To take another example, it can be argued that in certain circumstances there is no sense to saying that one person rather than another sees the true shade of a given colour, because the differences in what people appear to perceive is in part accounted for by variations in their perceptual organs and not uniquely by differences in the world outside them.

If we now apply these initial remarks to cultural relativism, we see that to establish the latter in its total form, the three following points would have to be argued for, in respect of each and every set of beliefs which men in this or that culture possess. First, that there is, or might be, an alternative and rival set of beliefs in another culture. Second, that there is no way of deciding rationally which culture — if any — is, or would be, correct. Third, that it does not even make sense to say that one culture is, or would be, uniquely correct — or that none at all is, or would be, correct.

Moreover, if the doctrine of total cultural relativism were to be established, it would follow that each and every expression of the form, 'this or that proposition is true', would have to be taken as an incomplete expression, requiring to be filled out by a reference to the culture, or cultures, within which alone the relevant proposition is, or could be, rightly asserted. At least this would be the case if the word 'true' continued to be employed at all. It would follow also that all claims to knowledge and all descriptions of reality would likewise have to be treated as incomplete claims and descriptions, needing mention to be made of this or that culture or cultures.

Some common but unsuccessful moves against total cultural relativism

There are several well-established moves against the doctrine of total cultural relativism. The first and most ambitious of these is to argue that the doctrine cannot coherently be stated, still less adequately defended; and the usual basis of this argument is the assertion that at some stage or other in attempting to state his case, the total relativist will make remarks which can only be interpreted as *universal* in their scope, and therefore as non-relative. For example, it is urged that the claim that all truths are relative cannot itself plausibly be intended as relative. For, what would be the point, it is asked, of the relativist's arguing at all, if he agreed from the outset that his own case is no more than one set of beliefs, relative to and determined by the culture to which he belongs?

However, this first kind of would-be refutation will not do, if only for the following reason. If its argument convinces anyone, it will convince only the already committed non-relativist. For only the latter is likely to accept that a claim intended to be universal in its application cannot be relative in its truth. The relativist himself, like the solipsist in similar circumstances and for similar reasons, will remain unmoved. Further, he will interpret whatever things are said against him as examples of alternative but not really rival claims: true within other philosophical cultures, false within his own.

The other moves most commonly attempted against the total cultural relativist consist largely in pointing out supposedly alarming features of his position. It is argued, for example, that he provides too ready a weapon for the intolerant and the dogmatist. What happier doctrine could the latter find, it is asked, than one which allows him never to be mistaken and always able to reject criticism as merely another's point of view? Or again it is argued that the relativist position, like that of the Wittgensteinian on forms of life, is too generous. It allows the defence of any or all beliefs to rest on the claim that they are acceptable as true within this or that culture. What is worse, there is no chance of curbing this liberality, since any attempt to do so may be dismissed as having force only within another, and in this case alien, culture.

Another consequence attributed to extreme cultural relativism is that it threatens the confidence of those whose job it is to hand on knowledge: parents, teachers and indeed all of us. Once we took knowledge itself to be culturally determined, it is argued, we would begin to doubt both the right and the point of our handing it on to others. After all, it is said, given the opportunity, our pupils might well prefer another culture and another knowledge.

These arguments from consequences are not without weight, but they can be met. It can be pointed out, for example, that the emotional unpalatability of results is never grounds for the rejection of a doctrine; or that to assume that the truth can have only pleasing outcomes is but wishful thinking. What then we are left with is this. The extreme cultural relativist is not open to head-on refutation, and the arguments against him from consequences are unable substantially to weaken his case.

Can nothing be done then? By way of convicting the kind of relativist who disclaims all onus of proof, nothing indeed can be done. He will interpret whatever is said against him as being in fact support for his own position, on the grounds that *ex hypothesi* whatever is said is relative. Like the believer willing to interpret hail or sunshine as equal evidence for divine providence, he is unassailable. But the price of his unassailability is high. He is not to be argued with, not because there are too powerful arguments in his favour, but because there are no arguments at all. He simply refuses to join in.

Things are not the same with the relativist who *does* claim to have arguments for his case. For it can be shown that he is mistaken, since there are no convincing arguments for total cultural relativism, and there could be none — as will shortly be made plain.

The 'comparative' argument in favour of total cultural relativism

To turn now to arguments used to *support* the doctrine of total cultural relativism.[2] First, there are two empirical arguments employed, one deriving from the comparative study of different cultures, the other from the internal study of this or that culture on its own.

In briefest outline, the strategy of the comparative argument is as follows. It begins by claiming to establish that there are many beliefs, both trivial and important, which differ radically and irreconcilably from culture to culture: beliefs such as those which concern the nature of the world, the nature of right and wrong, what should be valued, what is to count as a good piece of reasoning, the existence and properties of God. It then proposes the following explanation of these differences. Beliefs in themselves do not arise in isolation, but only within a given culture, dependent on it and fully determined by it. For this reason no beliefs have an intercultural validity of their own; even if they overlap, they still belong to and are relative to specific cultures.

This comparative argument is not really very compelling as a move in favour of *total* cultural relativism, since even if there are beliefs which do differ from culture to culture radically and irreconcilably, it can never be shown that *all* are on the same footing, that *all* are culturally relative.

There are several reasons for this, the first of which concerns the nature of belief itself.[3] If a person (or *mutatis mutandis* a culture) has a set of beliefs about the world, that person must, among other things, be aware of certain states of affairs, be able to distinguish one state of affairs from another, and assert or be prepared to assert (whether verbally or not) that this or that state of affairs obtains. But if we look closely at the last of these requirements, we see that it carries important implications. For, to make assertions is implicitly to exclude or deny the contradictions of those assertions. One can no more say 'yes' without implicitly excluding 'no' than one can refer to someone as 'fat' without at the same time implicitly refusing the ascription to him of 'thin'. Further, to appreciate the relation between assertion and denial is at the same time to appreciate the relation of implication: it is to grasp that if a belief is asserted, its contradictory *cannot* be asserted. And that is to have the beginnings of deductive logic.

This point can be made in a stronger form. It is argued from time to time that even the basic principles of logic are culturally determined and therefore culturally relative. However, this would entail the possibility that a culture might adopt, or already possess, a logic which wants even the principle of contradiction. But this would *not* be possible, since without that principle in operation assertions could not be made and beliefs could not be held. If a man were always, or even for the most part, to assert his beliefs while simultaneously conceding their denial, he would have no beliefs at all; assertion is ruled out by denial.

In the domain of beliefs then, there can be no alternative to the principle of contradiction, and no alternatives to the implications that it bears. And since in the absence of alternatives, the first premiss required to support relativism collapses, there are no grounds left for believing the principle of contradiction to be culturally relative.

Further, returning to the proposed comparative argument in favour of total cultural relativism, we can ask ourselves what is required if one set of beliefs is to be compared with another. Clearly what first is needed is that the one who does the comparing should *understand* the beliefs; that he should be able to 'translate' them. This is required of the cultural relativist above all, since he needs to be sure of having understood these or those cultures before he asserts that their differences really are radical; that he has not simply misunderstood them. But now we must go on to ask what are the minimum requirements of a person's understanding another's culture. Surely the answer is that the latter must have a set of referents and properties corresponding to those of the would-be understander. For if people of a culture different from our own were to acknowledge *nothing* that we could recognise — neither things nor properties — we could not begin matching our words and concepts with theirs. *A fortiori* we could not begin to judge how much their beliefs tie in with or depart from our own. For these reasons, neither fear nor hope is justified that people in other cultures may inhabit totally different 'realities' from ours, or possess entirely different sets of beliefs. For to understand a culture is chiefly to understand its beliefs, and the understanding of those beliefs demands in turn the inhabiting of a common world.

Perhaps we might go on to ask: *How* common a world? If we do, we can answer the question with reasonable accuracy if we bear in mind that the point at issue throughout has been the understanding of cultures belonging to *men*. For let us ask if any group of *men* could be discovered to differ totally from others in their beliefs. The answer surely is that they could not, since in such a case they would not be recognised as men at all.

This point provides us with an important clue and is worth pursuing, as it amounts to saying that before we can set about comparing cultures, we need first to be sure that the group of beings who possess them really are men. But do we know what men are?

Perhaps we cannot fully define what constitutes a group of men, but we can at least point to some of the properties we normally require of them. We require of them, for example, that they be able to recognise and act intelligently towards such material things as animal bodies, mountains and trees. If they could not recognise such objects, nor understand them enough to deal with them intelligently, they would not be able to recognise one another, nor consequently to form a human group; they would be able neither to recognise nor obtain items of food to keep themselves alive; they would be unable to recognise such things as rocks or boulders to avoid walking into them, and precipices to avoid falling over them.

More is to be said. As may be shown from any simple case, this requirement concerning material objects presupposes yet others. Let us consider, for example, the case of a man, however 'primitive', who is spearing fish in a river. To begin with, his doing this intelligently presupposes an awareness of causal regularities around him and a reliance on them. He must know at the minimum what sorts of causal interactions occur between his spear and the water, or between his spear and the fish. He must employ inductive reasoning, using his past experiences to anticipate the movements of the fish, to make allowances for the refractive properties of water, to adjust the throw of his spear. Even his observation of the fish carries with it intelligent assumptions. If a fish disappears behind a rock, for example, he will look for it to emerge, or if he turns away for a moment or two, he will not expect it to go out of existence. In short, any simple, intelligent activity presupposes major beliefs about the world: beliefs in the existence of causal connections, in the trustworthiness of the senses and of inductive reasoning, in the perdurance of material objects while unperceived.

What follows from all this is that if we allow intelligent interaction with material objects (including human bodies) to be a first requirement of men's counting as men, we can conclude that just as it proved impossible to allow of cultures in which beliefs might be held for the most part against or without the principle of contradiction, it now proves impossible to allow of those in which the recognition of material objects together with the use and awareness of causal connections and inductive reasoning would not be to the fore. We can conclude consequently that there is no case for saying that either the recognition of material objects or the use of causal and inductive reasoning is culturally relative.

The argument from change in favour of total cultural relativism

The second type of empirical argument used to support total cultural relativism may be stated in bold outline as follows. Cultures change. They change even in what those who belong to them consider to be their ultimate beliefs and principles. Second, there can be no means of deciding between changing sets of supposed ultimate principles or beliefs, precisely because what is held to be ultimate at any given period is *eo ipso* beyond appeal. Third, it follows from what has been said that it does not even make sense to say that this or that set of supposed ultimate beliefs at this or that period of time is correct or incorrect. The beliefs of any given culture then are radically relative, since even the most fundamental among them are subject to change.

11

As an illustration of this argument, those changes may be cited which are said to have occurred, or to be occurring, among the ultimate beliefs of our own — that is, Western — culture. It is argued, for example, that shifts have occurred which amount to the abandoning even of such principles as causality, excluded middle, identity and contradiction.

For the purpose of simplifying the assessment of this argument, we may safely suppose what many will deny: that certain shifts have indeed occurred. For, even if they have, they can do nothing to establish the case for total cultural relativism, as may be shown from examining any one of them.

Let us take as our example the principle of causality. There is no doubt that for long periods this principle was held to be both fundamental and exceptionless. It was used by scholastic philosophers attempting to prove the existence of God, and by Kant in his transcendental deduction where he argued that it was required for the existence of objects in the phenomenal world. But equally there is no doubt that, although the principle in its universal or exceptionless form is still adhered to by some scientists and philosophers (as it was by Einstein), it is rejected by others — on the grounds that it does not apply where human freedom is concerned, or that it does not fit in with quantum mechanics.

What follows from these points? It follows that it can with at least some plausibility be argued that the principle of causality, when interpreted as having universal application, is culturally relative. For if one person continues to subscribe to it and another rejects it, there appears to be no way even in principle of deciding between them. The first may argue that subatomic physics is not in a satisfactory state, and that a new physical theory needs to be sought, to dispense God from playing dice. The other may argue that since he sees no *a priori* grounds for holding to the principle of universal causality, his theory of free will or his theory of physics must be allowed to constitute a rejection of it.

To this sort of argument it might be objected that while we may have no means of deciding even in principle who is correct in the above conflict, it does not follow straight off that there is no *sense* to saying that the doctrine of universal and exceptionless causality is, or is not, correct. However, even if it *could* be shown that it makes no sense, and that the principle of universal causality is therefore culturally relative, little would have been gained on behalf of total cultural relativism. For to have shown that human cultures do not need a principle having *universal, exceptionless* application, is not to have shown that they do not need one having application *for the most part*. Clearly they do, for reasons that were given earlier and need now to be recalled only sketchily. Human intelligence and activity, it was argued, require an understanding of material objects, and this in turn requires a grasp of causal properties and regularities, since material objects of their essence are things with causal properties. Without the latter they could not interact with other objects (including men), could not be perceived, could not occupy space to the exclusion of others, and could not give rise to justifiable expectations and predictions.

If follows then that while there are some grounds for holding that the principle of exceptionless causality is culturally relative, there are none for holding the same concerning the principle having application for the most part. Nor could there be, for this second form of the causal principle is indispensable to human understanding. Further, these reflections on causality may be applied, *mutatis mutandis*, to the other fundamental principles of our culture. For example, even if it were shown that the traditional laws of thought need not apply in all cases, it could not be shown that they need not apply in most.

This brings us to the end of our consideration of the second empirical argument for cultural relativism, and to the conclusion that arguments drawn from the changes of one culture are no more successful than those which rely on the diversity of many.

An a priori argument

It will be useful to close this chapter with a brief look at an *a priori* argument sometimes used in favour of total cultural relativism. In substance this argument goes as follows. Since there could be no demonstration of the uniqueness of a set of fundamental principles, we must concede the possibility of the latter's being replaced. But this in turn is to concede the possibility of men's acquiring alternatives to any given set of principles; alternatives moreover of a rival and not merely complementary kind. Therefore, any set of fundamental principles is culturally relative.

This argument may be met at least in part by pointing out the following. If principles are to be replaced, this will be done either rationally or not. But we can never rationally replace our fundamental principles, for to do so would be to argue for new principles from within the framework of the old. For example, we could never argue rationally to adopt a replacement for the principle of contradiction, since to argue is to make assertions, to draw conclusions and so on, and the very doing of these things presupposes the principle of contradiction. For similar reasons, we could never argue for a replacement of the principle which allows the drawing of conclusions from premises, nor could we argue that the world of our common experience (of persons, tables and chairs) need no longer submit to the principle of causality for the most part. In short, there could be no rational means of transcending our fundamental principles, since the claim that their replacements were *rationally supported* would amount to the claim that the old principles were still in acceptance.

It might be urged against this that while such principles could not be replaced at once and together, there is no reason why they should not be replaced in piecemeal fashion, like the planks of Neurath's raft. But there is a reason, namely that such fundamental principles as those governing assertion, denial, contradiction, exclusion, implication and so on, do not resemble the planks of a raft. They cannot be separated. But this point has been argued already.

The alternative left us would be to replace our most basic principles by non-rational means: to migrate abruptly to a form of awareness in which there would be no beliefs, no assertions, no conclusions. But such a form of awareness — if we allow it to be intelligible at all — could have no bearing on the issue of total cultural relativism. For, given that it would not contain a set of beliefs, it could not be used as evidence for the existence of an alternative and rival set.

To summarise this chapter in a sentence. There are no persuasive reasons in support of total cultural relativism, and there could be none.

FURTHER READING

The following give a pretty wide introduction to the problems covered in this chapter, but inevitably parts of their contents extend to problems discussed later on. Those marked with an asterisk will best serve the beginner.

*Ayer, A.J. *Language, Truth and Logic,* London, 2nd ed., 1946, Chap. 4.
Barnes, B. "The Comparison of Belief-Systems: Anomaly Versus Falsehood", *Modes of Thought*, Finnegan, R. & Horton, R. (eds), London, 1973.
*Beattie, J. *Other Cultures,* London, 1964.
Beattie, J. "On Understanding Ritual", *Rationality*, Wilson, B. (ed.), Oxford, 1970.
Beattie, J. "Reason, Commitment and Dr. Trigg", *Philosophy*, 49 (1974), pp. 435-7.
Berger, P. & Luckmann, T., *The Social Construction of Reality*, Harmondsworth, 1967.
Berry, J.W. & Dasen, P.R. *Culture and Cognition,* London, 1974.
Bloor, D. *Knowledge and Social Imagery*, London, 1976.
Collingwood, R.G. *An Essay on Metaphysics*, Oxford, 1940.
Cooper, D.E. *Illusions of Equality,* London, 1980, Chap. 4.
*Gorbutt, D. "The New Sociology of Education", *Education for Teaching*, 89 (1972), pp. 3-11.
*Hollis, M. "The Limits of Irrationality", *Rationality*, B. Wilson (ed.), Oxford, 1970.
*Hollis, M. "Reason and Ritual", *Rationality*, B. Wilson (ed.), Oxford, 1970.
Hollis, M. "Witchcraft and Winchcraft", *Philosophy of the Social Sciences*, 2 (1972), pp. 89-103.
Horton, R. & Finnegan, R. *Modes of Thought,* London, 1973.
*Körner, S. *What is Philosophy?*, London, 1969, Part 4.
Körner, S. *Categorial Frameworks*, Oxford, 1970.
Körner, S. "Logic and Conceptual Change", *Conceptual Change*, G. Pearce & P. Maynard (eds), Dordrecht, 1973.
Lazari-Pawlowska, I. "On Cultural Relativism", *The Journal of Philosophy*, 67 (1970), pp. 577-584.
*Lukes, S. "Some Problems about Rationality", *Rationality,* B. Wilson (ed.), Oxford, 1970.

*Lukes, S. "On the Social Determination of Truth", *Modes of Thought,* R. Finnegan & R. Horton (eds), London, 1973.
*Lukes, S. "Relativism: Cognitive and Moral", *The Aristotelian Society,* supp. vol. 48 (1974), pp. 165-189.
*Mitchell, D. *An Introduction to Logic,* London, 1962, Chaps. 6 & 7.
*Newman, J. "Metaphysical Relativism", *Southern Journal of Philosophy,* 12 (1974), pp. 435-448.
Nielsen, K. "Appealing to Reason", *Inquiry,* 5 (1962), pp. 65-84.
Nielsen, K. "Wittgensteinean Fideism", *Philosophy,* 42 (1967), pp. 191-209.
*Nielsen, K. "Principles of Rationality", *Philosophical Papers,* 3 (1974), pp. 55-89.
*Nielsen, K. "Rationality and Relativism", *Philosophy of the Social Sciences,* 4 (1974), pp. 313-331.
*Nowell-Smith, P.H. "Cultural Relativism", *Philosophy of the Social Sciences,* 1 (1971), pp. 1-18.
Phillips, D.Z. *Faith and Philosophical Enquiry,* London, 1970.
Quine, W. "Two Dogmas of Empiricism", *From a Logical Point of View,* Harvard, 1953.
Remmling, G. *Towards the Sociology of Knowledge,* London, 1973.
Stark, W. *The Sociology of Knowledge,* London, 1958.
*Strawson, P. *Introduction to Logical Theory,* London, 1952, Chap. 1.
Trigg, R. *Reason and Commitment,* Cambridge, 1973.
Trigg, R. "Reason, Commitment and Social Anthropology", *Philosophy,* 51 (1976), pp. 219-222.
*Whorf, B.L. *Language, Thought and Reality,* J. Carroll (ed.), Cambridge, Mass., 1956.
*Winch, P. "The Idea of a Social Science", *British Journal of Sociology,* 7 (1956), pp. 18-33.
Winch, P. *The Idea of a Social Science,* Oxford, 1958.
*Winch, P. "Understanding a Primitive Society", *Religion and Understanding,* D.Z. Phillips (ed.), Oxford, 1967.
Wittgenstein, L. *Philosophical Investigations,* Oxford, 1958.
Wittgenstein, L. *On Certainty,* Oxford, 1969.
Wolfram, S. "Basic Differences of Thought", *Modes of Thought,* Finnegan, R. & Horton, R. (eds), London, 1973.
Wright Mills, C. "Language, Logic and Culture", *American Sociological Review,* 4 (1939), pp. 670-680.
Young, M. *Knowledge and Control,* London, 1971.

CHAPTER 2
CULTURAL RELATIVISM AND THE NATURAL SCIENCES

In Chapter 1 it was argued that neither the fundamental principles of logic nor the basic causal framework within which our experience is structured can with reason be described as culturally relative: more briefly, that what henceforward will be referred to as men's *commonsense* beliefs are not determined by the individual cultures to which they belong. What needs from now on to be done is to examine the more complex and developed areas of human knowledge and belief, and to ask whether there are good reasons for saying that these are culturally relative.

The best area to start with would seem to be the natural sciences, since there is a fairly widespread and not implausible view that for the most part the latter are no more than systematic extensions of 'commonsense' anyway.

Over a fairly long period in modern times, the natural sciences have been taken pretty solidly to be the one area in which, if in any, men are able to come to grips with reality and make progress in discovering what the world is really like. Further, and as a result of this, the natural sciences — often referred to simply as 'science' — have long been accepted by many as the ideal paradigm of knowledge.

In spite of this traditionally high standing, in recent years and from several directions at once, 'science' has increasingly come under attack. It has been accused of bringing more harm than good to men; of having become little more than a tool in the hands of politicians and ideologists; of pretending to furnish ultimate explanations of the universe while in fact putting forward only unexplained regularities. In addition, and of immediate relevance to this chapter, the criticism has been made that science (to use from now on the simplified appellation) comprises sets of beliefs which are no more than relative to certain cultures or sub-cultures; that there is no such thing as science *tout court*, but only Western science, bourgeois science, Marxist science or whatever, and that all of these are sets of beliefs which consequently can have no claim to acceptance beyond their respective cultures.

It is this last criticism that the present chapter will attempt to meet, and in order to do this it will need first to give an account of the nature and methods of science. This unfortunately will not be an easy task, since the nature of science at the moment is the focus of a great deal of controversy, and considerable changes have taken place in men's views of it. Perhaps then the best way to proceed will be as follows: first, to examine the once traditional and still popular view of science as a body of knowledge revealing to us in a simple and straightforward manner what reality is like; second, to look at the principal rival to this once traditional view; third, to attempt to draw up a set of moderate and, it is to be hoped, generally acceptable observations on the nature of science; finally, and in the light of this, to examine the claims of relativism.

Naive Inductivism

The view of science which was once traditional and is still often stated outright in textbooks is usually referred to as naive inductivism. In broad outline it is associated principally with the name of Francis Bacon, and its main tenets are the following.

Science essentially consists in assembling facts which are based upon, and in some manner derived from, the use of the senses. The scientist carefully observes, does experiments to provide sources for new observations, varies the conditions in which he observes (in order to avoid recording coincidental occurrences), and in addition makes careful and precise measurements. When in this way he has collected sufficient information, he draws conclusions from what he has observed and these conclusions take the form of general statements; statements such as: all gases expand when heated, all metals conduct electricity, any two particles of matter attract each other with a force proportional to the product of their masses and inversely proportional to the square of the distances between them.

This process just described, of drawing general conclusions from sets of particular observations, is usually referred to as the process of enumerative induction. The scientist observes, for example, that in a large number of cases metals expand when heated; he then widely varies the conditions in which he makes his observations, discovers no case of a metal which does not expand, and so draws the conclusion inductively that all metals expand when heated.

Observation, which in the above way is said to form the basis of the conclusions of science, is also said on the whole to be able directly to reveal reality to us. Our senses, in other words, are held to show in some immediate fashion what the world in itself is like, independently of its observers. For this reason, it is urged, and because it does not attempt to go much beyond the findings of the senses, science is able to provide us with certainty (or as near certainty as matters) concerning the nature of the world.

When the scientist starts his observations, the naive inductivist continues, he does so in a manner which is open and unbiased. That is, first he makes his observations with careful impartiality and then he draws his conclusions. He does not start out with conclusions and subsequently allow them to dictate such things as what he is to observe, where he is to observe, or what he is to count as an observation in the first place. His observations in short are open, free and neutral, in no way dictated to by preconceived theories or conclusions.

Given that science is this kind of steady amassing of plain facts, its progress is unbroken and rectilinear. It suffers no reversals, no collapses, no crises comparable to those of theology, philosophy or history. Its very simplicity assures it unimpeded success.

From what was said earlier concerning observations and their way of leading to generalised conclusions, it follows that what counts as an explanation in science is the demonstration of how this or that particular fact or kind of fact comes under a generalisation already inductively established. We can explain, say, that cobalt expands when heated by arguing that it expands because it is a metal; and in turn we can explain that metals expand when heated by appealing to generalisations concerning the increased motion of their constituent molecules or atoms.

Finally, this process of observing, collating, generalising and then explaining in terms of generalisations, is what is meant by the rational process of science. That is, if we wish to determine whether this or that scientist has proceeded rationally at any given juncture, we need but look at his observational findings, conclusions and explanations. If, and only if, he has kept to the rules of procedure outlined above, he has acted rationally.

So much for the view of the naive inductivist. It is a view which is thoroughly objectivist, since it takes the conclusions of science to be simply generalisations from what the senses are able directly to reveal concerning the nature of reality. It does not allow that the way the latter appears to the scientist is structured or altered by his organs of sense, prior beliefs, presuppositions or anything else. Reality appears, it holds, as reality is.

Criticisms of naive inductivism

The naive inductivist view as above briefly stated has been subjected to a number of criticisms recently, principally on the following lines.

First, it has been pointed out that many of the central concepts of science are not observational in the way that naive inductivism implies. Thus, for example, the concepts of *force, field, inertia* and *mass* do not apply to the sorts of things that come under the senses in the way that laboratory benches and geiger-counters come under them.

More important, observation is only one among many factors that are and should be given weight in the assessment of scientific claims. Theories may well be, and often are, given preference not in virtue of the range and accuracy of their predicted or otherwise associated observations, but (among other things) because they have simplicity and elegance, because they have fewer anomalies than their rivals, because they result in substantial metaphysical and conceptual gains. Thus in extreme cases theories are persevered with even when the weight of observational evidence against them is greater than that in their favour.[1]

Again, while observation plays a more important part in science than in most forms of knowledge, the observation in question does not constitute the sort of direct confrontation with reality that the naive inductivist would have us believe. For, on all occasions when men observe, their own minds contribute something to the immediate object of their observation. To illustrate this with an example which may be adapted and extended to all the senses, when two persons are subjected to the same sort of visual stimuli and receive the same sort of retinal image, they will nonetheless sometimes perceive quite different 'things', in keeping with the differences of their background experiences, expectations, stores of knowledge, assumptions, presuppositions and even modes of conceptualising. In short, when men perceive or observe, what they perceive or observe is the joint outcome of what there is in the world and what they themselves bring to it.[2] It follows that there is no such thing as neutral observation, no such thing as a direct, unmediated confrontation with reality.

The second principal criticism levelled against naive inductivism is that it attributes certainty to the findings of science. But such an attribution, it is said, is unwarranted, since the observational statements which are advanced as premises of scientific conclusions can no more guarantee the truth of those conclusions than the facts presented to juries can guarantee the guilt or innocence of this or that defendant. The history of trials shows only too clearly that the verdicts of juries, however well these are informed and instructed, are on occasion wrong. The history of science shows just as clearly that the 'findings' of scientists are on occasion wrong.[3] Science then cannot be said to bring certainties.

There is a point that is often added here, on the grounds that it arises from the last two criticisms taken together. This is that the naive inductivist considers the observational premises of scientific conclusions to be independent of those conclusions. But, for the reasons already given, it is argued that they are not. What the scientist observes is in fact determined by his already existing theories and interests, and therefore his observations are 'theory-laden'. For example, what a good biologist observes through his microscope is in great measure dependent on the theoretical and other beliefs that he brings with him. Like everyone else he in part sees what he expects to see, and what his beliefs, theories and ways of conceptualising enable him to see.[4] To put this in a more general way, what a scientist or anyone else observes is necessarily observed under some description or other. But descriptions are embedded in and are functions of networks of concepts, theories and beliefs. They are not the results of what one might call 'raw' observations.

The third criticism brought against naive inductivism is that even in cases where a scientist may very properly be said to draw generalised conclusions

19

from observed phenomena, his method of doing this is often quite removed from that described by the naive inductivist. This is because it is often plainly unnecessary to have a large number of observations to support a generalised conclusion. A small number is all that is needed when the generalisation is one which fits straight off into an already existing and successful framework of beliefs.[5] Similarly, an exception here or there is often justifiably brushed aside, on the grounds that there is some quite obvious explanation for it, but one which in the context is not worth pursuing.

The fourth criticism is one which again follows from what has been said, and concerns the nature of scientific explanation. It is that because so much of science cannot accurately be described as generalising from observational facts, scientific explanation in turn cannot be held to consist simply in showing that this or that explanandum is an instance of a general law. Thus, for example, when the theory of evolution through natural selection is used to explain similarities across species, it cannot be said that nothing more is appealed to than a set of generalisations drawn from observed occurrences. Indeed biologists might have made observations and generalised from them indefinitely without coming up with a theory such as that of evolution through natural selection. What is more, if the proper task of science were no more than the drawing of general conclusions from observations, the greater part of what traditionally has been practised under its name might have to be dismissed as unwarranted, as the interference of the imagination or of metaphysical and conceptual interests.[6]

A final point made against naive inductivism is that in its more popularised forms it tends to speak as if there could be no serious scientific explanations without precise measurement. But this is not so. For while precise measurement is of great use in most if not in all scientific investigations, it does not have to form part of the resulting theories and explanations themselves. Thus, for example, the explanation of diseases by reference to viruses is perfectly intelligible and requires of itself no mention of precise measurement. The same may be said of the explanations of such things as geological formations, similarities and developments among animal species, and the origin of the cosmos itself. While precise measurement may play a useful auxiliary role in these explanations, it would not seem to constitute a part of their essence.

Falsificationism

The most striking and clear-cut challenge to naive inductivism lies in the doctrine of falsificationism, a theory which shares with its rival the attraction of simplicity. In its general features it is the contribution of Karl Popper to the philosophy of science.

This doctrine of falsificationism begins by rejecting the view of science as a collection of certainly known facts, based upon and inductively established by observation; and it does this because it holds that induction can never seriously be thought to justify the conclusions of science, nor *a fortiori* to bring certainty. The reasons behind this conviction are chiefly those of the philosopher Hume: that as far as logic goes anything in the world of experience can follow anything, and that all attempts to justify induction by appeals to experience are bound to be circular.

While in this manner rejecting induction and consequently inductivism, the falsificationist proposes as an alternative that the proper method of science is to advance hypotheses having the status merely of conjectures; and he adds that these latter may be arrived at no matter how, that their origin is of no importance. What matters rather is what befalls them once they are arrived at. Having rejected induction, the falsificationist cannot now justly propose that the task of the scientist is to set about substantiating his conjectures inductively. What he does instead is to suggest that the scientist's task is to submit his conjectures to a series of tests in which they are exposed to the risk of being overthrown. In other words, what he proposes as the proper goal of the scientist is not that he establish that this or that given conjecture is true, but that he try his utmost to show it to be false. If he succeeds in this, the conjecture in question is at once to be set aside and an alternative looked for. If he fails, and for as long as he fails, the conjecture is to be retained and made use of. Thus, for example, we might imagine a physicist conjecturing that the nature of light is wave-like — a supposition which enables him to explain such phenomena as interference and polarisation. For the time being he continues with and makes use of this conjecture; but then, after assiduously putting it to the test, he comes across such falsifying evidence as the photoelectric effect. In such an event his proper course is at once to abandon his conjecture, and to search for an alternative.

A related point here is that if a conjecture turns out to be of such a kind that it cannot and could not even in principle be shown to be false, it follows that however useful and important it is as an hypothesis of a metaphysical or some other sort, it is not scientific. In other words, the characteristic of falsifiability is what distinguishes science from other kinds of intellectual enterprise.

Given what so far has been said, there are no reasons in theory why on the view of the falsificationist the conjectures of science should not be true and accurate descriptions of reality as it is in itself. But while this sort of correspondence to reality is *possible* on falsificationist premises, neither scientist nor anyone else could ever have adequate grounds for believing it actually to obtain. For the scientist with propriety can only hold that his present conjectures have not been shown to be false. He cannot claim that in the future they will not be refuted, and indeed it is his task to do all in his power to ensure that they will be. On the other hand, it does not follow from this that there are no rational means of preferring one conjecture to another. On the contrary, the grounds for choice are often perfectly clear. One conjecture may, for example, have wider explanatory power than its rivals; it may fit more easily into already existing frameworks of belief; it may require fewer conceptual revisions; it may yield a greater number of useful predictions.[7]

Further, it does not obviously follow from the tentativeness of his conjectures that the scientist may not justly *aim* at acquiring a true and accurate description of reality. For he may argue with at least some plausibility that through his processes of conjecture and refutation he draws progressively closer to a description of reality; even if he can never have adequate grounds for thinking that he has fully achieved it. He can at least be sure of having ruled out much that is false.

This in brief outline is the doctrine of falsificationism. Clearly its conception of rationality is different from that of naive inductivism, since according to the falsificationist a scientist is rational not when he draws unalterable generalisations from particular observations (an impossible achievement) and then uses these as explanantia, but when he advances explanatory hypotheses which are derived no matter whence, and which he both knows to be refutable and strives to refute. It should also be clear from what has been said that while the doctrine of falsificationism is in some ways an objectivist doctrine, it is not so whole-heartedly objectivist as naive inductivism. For while it holds that refuted conjectures both genuinely tell us something of what reality is not, and at the same time enable a progression towards a true grasp of how things positively are, by contrast with naive inductivism it does not hold that all acceptable scientific claims are matters of certain and direct revelation of reality.

Criticisms of falsificationism

As was the case with naive inductivism, there are several major criticisms that are made of falsificationism.

First, falsificationism, it is argued, accords too large and important a place to observation in the supposed processes of science. For its most central tenet is that when conjectures have been made, they are to be put to the test of observation: if they clash with the latter they are to be rejected; if not they are to be persevered with. However, as was pointed out in the discussion of inductivism, observation is not the only, and on rare occasions is not even the most important consideration entering into the assessment of scientific claims.[8] The scientist must be prepared to consider in addition such things as conceptual economy, metaphysical plausibility, elegance and balance of advantage in what concerns the handling of anomalies. In other words, scientific hypotheses and theories are not always rejected because they conflict with observational findings. Sometimes they are rejected because they put intolerable strains on non-observational parts of our belief-systems; sometimes, at the other end of the scale, they are retained in spite of their conflicts with observation.[9]

A second and related criticism is that when there is a clash between a conjecture and observation, falsificationism assumes that it is the conjecture which is refuted thereby, not the observation. But this assumption is not warranted. For sometimes it is clearly the supposed observational findings, or perhaps the theories in which these are embedded, which are at fault.[10] Consequently there is no rule in advance for saying what is to be persevered with, conjecture or observation.

A third and again related criticism is that hypotheses or conjectures in science do not exist in isolation; they are always firmly set in a corpus of theories, beliefs and suppositions. Further, when they are tested, assumptions have to be made concerning the appropriatenes and reliability of the procedures in train and the trustworthiness of the testing-equipment involved.[11] For these reasons, when observation clashes with a conjecture, the proper course for the scientist may well be the rejection not of the conjecture but of a theory or some other member of the background beliefs and assumptions. It is misleading then to describe the method of science as the putting forward of conjectures and the subsequent attempt to refute them, since this at the very least suggests that conjectures are isolable units, open singly to testing and refutation. In fact they stand or fall in the company of other beliefs and assumptions.

A fourth and brief criticism is that as an account of what all science is about, the doctrine of falsificationism is counter-intuitive. To bring this out with an example, when the anatomist undertakes to give a detailed description of the structures of human or other bodies, it is implausible to suggest that he is, or ought to be, aiming merely at showing that this or that conjecture is false. Because of this, some philosophers have wished to claim that anatomy and other such subjects are not really parts of science at all. However, there are no obvious and compelling reasons for accepting this kind of revision in terminology.

A final criticism of falsificationism is that it does not accord well with much of the past practice of science. Theories or conjectures have simply not always been abandoned in the face of conflicting observational evidence, however powerful, and it is just as well for the history and progress of science that this has been so. Thus, Newton's theory of planetary motion was not abandoned because of such observations as those concerning the perihelion of Mercury, nor was Darwin's theory abandoned because of its conflict with the apparently better observationally supported thermodynamics of his time. No doubt it is possible to say that the clinging to either theory was in the circumstances irrational, but surely it is more plausible to argue that science is a less simple undertaking and process than falsificationism is willing to allow.

Modifications to falsificationism

A number of attempts have been made by philosophers such as Imre Lakatos to preserve the principal features and underlying spirit of falsificationism while overcoming its weaknesses, especially those weaknesses which lie in assuming on the one hand that all conjectures in science should be open to testing and revision, and on the other hand that all such conjectures are testable singly, rather than as parts of wider beliefs. These attempts have usually taken the form of arguing that scientists work and should work within a framework, comprising a set of fundamental beliefs which are not put to the test, and a set of lower-level beliefs which are and should be tested. Scientists, as the current terminology goes, work within research programmes or traditions, pursuing their investigations within boundaries which are left unchallenged. For example, astronomers working within the research tradition of Newtonian mechanics leave unquestioned its basic laws of motion and gravity, but do not leave unquestioned such things as the path of this or that planet, or the accuracy of the findings of this or that instrument.

However, there are difficulties in spelling out what is to count as a research programme or tradition, and difficulties in saying what precisely might be acceptable procedures within one. Further, there are too many scientists who cannot seriously be said to have worked within one tradition anyway. For these and other reasons (later to be touched on), it seems better to abandon the quest for a unitary model of the procedures of science and instead to acknowledge and bring out the latter's complexity.

The discussions in previous sections have already drawn attention to most of the features of science which conjointly ensure its complexity, but it will be useful now to systematise and codify what has been said, especially as much of it has been said only indirectly. This will best be done by setting down two series of points concerning the nature of science and its methods, the first dealing with what cannot properly be said, the second with what can.

What science is not

Science is not simply an accumulation of observed facts and generalisations drawn from the latter. To take examples at random, Galileo's theory of circular inertia, Newton's theory of rectilinear inertia and Dalton's theory of atoms are good cases of hypotheses which go well beyond what is observed and cannot be reduced to statements about what is observed, nor *a fortiori* to generalisations from such statements.

The claims, hypotheses and theories of science do not, any more than any other claims about the world, result from a direct confrontation between the senses and reality. There would seem to be little or nothing which might be described as unmediated, neutral observation, recording in faithful, camera-like fashion the details of reality. When we perceive or observe the world, interpretation takes place, in such a way that an identical set of physiological data recorded in the senses of two persons, or of the same person on two separate occasions, is often interpreted in quite different ways.[12] This is because what men perceive is in part determined by such influences as their organs of sense, prior beliefs, language, understanding, education and training.

This does not mean that there is no common world of referents from which science can get going. It has already been argued (in Chapter 1) that there is, and the point will be returned to later.

Observation is not the only important element in the formation, acceptance and rejection of scientific theories. Not infrequently such considerations as metaphysical gain, conceptual advantage and simplicity enter in. For reasons of this kind, scientists have at times given thought to such things as the possibility of action at a distance, the intelligibility of absolute simultaneity, the intelligibility of four-dimensional space-time, the acceptability of creation *ex nihilo*. Or they have taken theories on trust which have had little more than simplicity to recommend them against their rivals; as was the case for a long period in the history of the Copernican view of the heavens.

No single piece of evidence purporting either to confirm or to refute a theory is to be taken as decisive. It is always possible that the supposed confirming or refuting evidence will itself shortly be dismissed as unsatisfactory, or that means will be found of explaining it away and allowing the theory in question to be continued with.[13] And there are of course often good reasons for wishing to continue with a given theory; it may, for example, have an impressive record in making useful predictions, or it may have an unusual range of explanatory power.

The related point may be made (already spelled out in the last section) that just as pieces of evidence are not to be considered singly as decisive, so hypotheses or theories are not to be thought of as confirmed or refuted on their own. They are to be seen as parts of wider theoretical systems or networks of belief.

However strong the evidence is in support or confirmation of a theory, it never guarantees it against subsequent revision or even outright rejection. This is simply to say that the theories of science are not arrived at deductively; their evidence always underdetermines them, leaving open the possibility of revisions or replacements.

There is no single kind of explanation in science which can properly serve as a model for all. Some explanations are appeals to well-established and observed regularities; others to the existence of items observable in principle but not observed in fact; yet others to items and forces which even in principle cannot be observed. Again, some explanations appeal to universal, exceptionless laws; others to statistical probabilities. It may well be a sheer mistake, then, to look for a model to fit them all.

The progress of science is not rectilinear. Many theories in the past have been revised or rejected, and on occasion some of those which had been

25

pushed aside have managed to return, in modified form, to oust their previously successful rivals. This, for example, was the case with the wave and particle theories of light. In similar fashion many of our own preferred theories are likely to be revised or rejected at some period in the future, and possibly some of those which we have cast aside will be resurrected and reinstated, again in modified form, by future generations.

There is no set of rules, and probably could be no set of rules, enabling scientists to arrive at theories 'mechanically'; that is, by a series of previously known steps. In some cases theories are arrived at by virtual stabs in the dark. In other cases it seems fairly obvious what suggested them. For example, when we look back on Harvey's solution to the problem of how the blood flows, it seems obvious that the solution came to him when and because he noticed features of the body's functioning which bear similarities to those of mechanical pumps. However, these apparently obvious cases provide us with no useful rule for arriving at theories. At best they encourage us to look for illuminating analogies, and there are no good rules for how to set about that. We might as well be told from the start to be creative.

From the points which have already been made it follows that there is, and could be, no one criterion for what is to count as the next rational step in any given scientific discussion or investigation. What is rational depends on balancing the demands of logic, observation, simplicity, metaphysical plausibility and all the other elements referred to from time to time above. For this reason, deciding what is rational in a scientific context is often as lacking in simplicity as deciding what is rational in economics or politics.

If it be asked how we are to distinguish science from other areas of human enquiry, it must be replied that there is no single criterion. Science is distinguished from everyday enquiries, for example, by being more systematic, and from such things as metaphysical enquiry by relying more heavily on observation.

What can more positively be said about science

Science is descriptive, in many if not most areas. Thus anatomy, botany, biology and even parts of physics are concerned (among other things) with description: with making plain the structures and mechanisms of such things as animal bodies, plants and pieces of magnetic substances.

Against this sort of assertion it is sometimes protested that science — 'real science' — is not properly concerned with description at all, but with explanation; and that when scientists in fact engage in describing, they do so merely on their way to formulating theories and explanations. But this view of science is unduly restrictive. For many (if not most) scientists obviously do take an interest in finding out what things are like — what their properties and behaviour are — and this interest is not necessarily the preliminary to a search for explanations; even if in fact it usually is. Furthermore, surely the explanations of science themselves are based upon claims which are meant to be truly descriptive of such things as regularities in the world; and even bearing in mind that men are not able directly to confront reality, there is no reason why their claims should not be accepted as descriptive in this way. In short, these and other kinds of explanation in science, far from excluding descriptions, are seen to depend upon them.

This does not mean, however, that all the propositions of science need to be construed as descriptive; even when their language is that of description and when they are originally intended as such. On the contrary, there are cases where it can be more reasonable to interpret scientific claims rather as referring to iconic models than as furnishing literal descriptions. Examples of such cases are to be found in Faraday's references to lines of magnetic force, in the claims of more recent physicists that space itself is affected by the presence of magnets, and again in the talk by recent physicists and astronomers of the curvature of space to explain the phenomena of gravitation. Indeed it could fairly be argued that not even the descriptions implicit in the use of iconic models are at stake here, on the grounds that it is possible neither to visualise nor to construct a physical model of the curvature or any other internal modification of space.

While, for reasons already given, observation is not the only important element in the procedures of science, it is nonetheless entirely central to them. There are few cases in the history of science where advances have not been accompanied or preceded by a considerable quantity of close and organised observation.

While there are severe objections to the doctrine of falsificationism as an exclusive account of the methodology of science, this should not lead us to overlook or to minimise the part played by falsification and refutation in science's progress and development. There is no doubt, for example, that the Michelson-Morley refutation of the theory of ether contributed to important developments in physics and astronomy, as did Galileo's refutation earlier (thanks to Jupiter and its moons) of the Aristotelian theory of the spheres.

While confirmation through observation, because of the very nature of non-deductive reasoning, can never guarantee the correctness of theories and hypotheses, it is certainly of importance in strengthening them; that is, in rendering them more plausible. Thus, to return to examples cited earlier, for a long time the existence of viruses was assumed, for the sake of explaining certain sorts of diseases. When at length these viruses came to be observed, through electron-microscopes, this greatly strengthened their claim to existence and their claim to being causes of the diseases in question. Similar kinds of remarks may be made of the existence of Mendel's 'factors' as causes of inherited traits; and, at the level of less observational theories, Newton's laws of motion and gravity were conspicuously strengthened by the discovery of Neptune, and Einstein's general theory of relativity by the discovery of the predicted bending of light.

27

Although enumerative induction cannot be accepted as the whole method of discovery and progress in science, it should not for that reason be dismissed altogether. For, to return again to the example of Mendel and the inheritance of characteristics, the 'laws' which he enunciated were the outcome of enumerative induction; yet surely it would be odd on this account to deny them a place in science or to allow it to them only on the strength of their being subsequently confirmed by the findings of microbiology.

In fact there is a reasonable case for saying that a very great deal of what counts as scientific knowledge was arrived at by the process of enumerative induction (Boyle's law, Snell's law, Charles' law, and so on), and that the latter therefore has played a crucial part in the progress of science — whatever the philosophical difficulties facing its justification.

While all observations which contribute to science may be said to be theory-laden, there are importantly different levels of their being so.

At a lowest level it is true that all observations are theory-laden, for a reason that has now been made clear several times over: namely that whenever and whatever we observe, in science or elsewhere, we always carry some background beliefs and assumptions with us. Because of this, our commonsense observations, as much as those which are more narrowly scientific, are theory-laden.

However, while for these reasons no given observations are entirely free and independent of theoretical beliefs, it does not follow that they cannot be independent of this or that theory which eventually they come to support. This point may be brought out in the following way. When a raw layman observes that rocks are stratified and contain 'fossils', that water evaporates when heated, that magnets attract iron filings and so on, his observations are certainly affected and even selected and guided to some degree by his commonsense theories; by contrast, they are not coloured or directed in advance by theories of science. But when he learns about and absorbs some of the relevant theories of geology, biology and physics, his observations of rocks, fossils and the rest begin to be modified, selected and directed by his newly acquired theories. And thus a sort of hierarchy of theory-ladenness is built up. A given set of observations can be theory-laden with respect to one theory (relatively low in the hierarchy) but quite free with respect to another (higher up). And as an observer acquires new and more complex theories, his observations become hierarchically more theory-laden, while remaining independent or neutral in respect of those theories (actual or possible) which he has not yet acquired.

From this it should be clear that those philosophers are wrong who argue that observations can never be separated out from the theories which they support, on the grounds that observations are always theory-laden. For the plain truth is that while all observations are theory-laden, observations are not laden with all theories.

A point closely related to what has just been said is that while many observations made in science are theory-guided and theory-selected, many also are not. For example, when scientists first began to make observations through microscopes, and so discovered the world of micro-organisms, there is no reason to suggest that their observations were specifically guided and selected by this or that theory. On the contrary, there is a sense in which initially they were 'just observing' — though their observations were of course theory-laden in the manner discussed in the last few paragraphs. In fact, on occasion considerable strides have been made in physics and elsewhere thanks to quite undirected observations; as was the case with Roentgen's photographic plates, or with Oersted's magnet and electric currents. In short, it is not true, though it seems at times to have been suggested, that no significant observations are made in science which are not pre-selected and guided by a specific and already formulated theory.

If the question is asked, What is the aim of science?, there would appear to be no single answer. Sometimes its aim is description; sometimes explanation; sometimes generalisation; sometimes prediction and utility; sometimes the resolution of metaphysical or conceptual problems. Again, individuals have different aims and purposes in doing science. One may be looking for the truth; another looking to make predictions; another to gain personal power or prestige; yet another to achieve political and social goals. And from this it follows that, while the individual's motives and interests do not affect the status of his findings, observations and theories, they can and often do affect the area in which he pursues his career and interests.

That concludes the twofold series of points on the nature and methodology of science, and the view that emerges from them is a substantial theory in its own right. In essence it insists on the complexity of the processes of science, and it brings to the fore the major constituents of that complexity. To summarise in a sentence or two, its argument is that when a theory in science is under assessment, it may be favoured or rejected on more grounds than one, and that no single kind of ground takes automatic precedence over any other. Thus a theory may draw strength (or be weakened, *mutatis mutandis*) from one or more of the following: from its internal structure — that is, from such things as its inner logical coherence, simplicity and elegance; from its compatibility with, or from the corroboration it brings to, related theories; from its manner of fitting in with background hypotheses, beliefs and assumptions — whether scientific, commonsense, logical, conceptual or even metaphysical; from the effects which it produces on other areas of thought, such as the simplicity or conceptual economy that it brings to them; from its comparison with rival theories; from the observational findings which support it; from the proportion of outstanding problems that it succeeds in solving; from the wealth of its predictions; from the promise which it seems to hold for the future.

The virtue of this view, with its emphasis on complexity, is that it manages to make sense of science without sharply divorcing it from other areas of human reasoning. More important still, it provides an account of scientific rationality which is able to agree with the facts and the course of history.

Science and cultural relativism

Philosophers have sometimes wished to argue, as has now been mentioned more than once, that all men's beliefs and concepts, including those which fall within science, are creations of the mind, and therefore in some sort matters of convention. Sociologists have at times advanced the analogous thesis that the beliefs and concepts of science are no more than the products of the societies within which they arise. Ideologists in turn have viewed science as a reflection of the values, aims and desires of their opponents, and have accordingly referred to it in such terms as 'Jewish', 'Marxist' or 'Western bourgeois'. Finally, even the non-committed layman on occasion is heard to suggest that we should hesitate to present science as objectively true, or to impose upon others what are perhaps the values, conventions and prejudices of this or that peculiar society or culture.

To examine whether these views, or any of them, are right, it will be useful to group scientific claims and their related concepts into the following separate kinds: those which concern what men observe or have observed; those which concern what men do not and have not observed, but could in principle observe; those which concern what men do not, have not, and could not even in principle observe.

1. Scientific claims concerning what men observe or have observed

Many if not most claims of this sort may be said *prima facie* to be made as the result of observations with the unaided senses, and they include much of botany, anatomy, meteorology, biology, chemistry and even physics. To return to Mendel's findings on the recurring properties of his peas, these were based on observations of this sort, as were the early descriptions of recurring patterns among iron filings in the presence of magnets.

Concerning claims of this kind there is not likely to be much disagreement or rivalry among cultures. Moreover, if and when disagreements do occur, the method of settling them is surely not in dispute: it is simply to appeal to further observations. But then, as was argued in Chapter 1, where there is an agreed way of judging between rival claims to the truth, there are no grounds for considering these to be relative. We know in advance that one of them is false. Thus if some zoologists assert and others deny that cats will interbreed with rabbits, we know in advance that one party will certainly turn out to be wrong.

For reasons which have already cropped up here and there in the course of this chapter, not everyone will be happy with this brief conclusion. Some will object, for example, that observation is not neutral and intersubjectively judgeable in the way that seems here to be assumed, since it is in part determined by prior beliefs, expectations and the like; others that the conclusions of science are underdetermined by the evidence supporting them and are therefore always open to rivals; others again that the observations used to support scientific claims are usually selected and directed in advance, and are therefore likely to be neither neutral nor objective.

For the purposes of the present context, the substance of these and kindred objections may be conceded. For whether or not they themselves are valid, any use of them to support cultural relativism certainly is not. Thus it may be conceded that observing with the unaided senses is not an unmediated recording of the way things are, and that the conclusions of science are both underdetermined by their supporting evidence and directed in advance by theoretical considerations. But it does not follow from this that the observational conclusions of science are culturally relative.

If there is any doubt on this point, a return can be made to what was said in Chapter 1. It was argued there that men inhabit a world of common referents and properties, without which they could not be recognised as human nor be able to distinguish their fellows as such. It was further argued that in this world of common items to engage thoughtfully in activities of even the most obvious kind — such as spearing fish in water — men must both possess and be familiar with a range of concepts for material objects and properties, and at the same time command a considerable ability in the use of drawing inductive (that is, non-deductive) conclusions. It was then argued that this kind of basic activity, together with its accompanying beliefs, already presupposes a substantial amount of 'theory', in that it demands a prior grasp of such things as the stability of sequences among events, the perdurance of material objects, and the general predictability of the contents of the world. It was argued finally that because these sorts of beliefs, assumptions and activities are, and have to be, common to all groups of men, they cannot with plausibility be thought of as culturally relative.

These arguments may now be applied in the following way to the issue of cultural relativism and the observations of science. The observing of such things as plants, peas, bones or iron filings, is no different in kind from the observing of fish, spears or water; nor is the process of predicting and reasoning inductively in the one case any different from that in the other. It follows that the descriptive observational parts of botany, biology, chemistry and the rest, are *continuous with commonsense* (using 'commonsense' with the meaning introduced at the beginning of this chapter), and for that reason are no more culturally relative than the latter itself. For, to return to a consideration of the objections mentioned earlier, if observation in science is not an uninterpreted awareness of reality, and if its conclusions are underdetermined, selected and directed, the selfsame is true of the observations of commonsense.

A similar argument may be advanced to meet the accusation that the observational claims of science are value-laden. Indeed they are, but no more than the claims of commonsense. The primitive hunter, engaged in spearing his fish, carefully observes and carefully draws conclusions; and when he does so it is because he chooses and values these procedures — at least with an eye to their results. But if these evaluative components of commonsense in no way render it culturally relative, as clearly they do not, the parallel components of 'observational science' cannot fairly be said to render that culturally relative either.

What has been said so far concerns scientific beliefs resting on observations with the unaided senses. It may now be added, and briefly argued for, that no difference of consequence arises when observations are made with the help of instruments.

Where optical instruments are concerned, this would seem to be pretty obvious, since there is no plausibility in the suggestion that optical lenses (always) significantly distort our vision of reality; in too many cases we are able to carry out independent checks to prove the contrary. For example, we are able to examine the landscape through binoculars at a distance of many kilometres, and later on, as we draw close, check our findings with the eyes alone. An even more obvious example lies in the use of spectacles: men only wear these because they believe them able to correct the distortions of their naked vision. And similar sorts of things may be said concerning hearing-aids and instruments designed to help the other senses.

Where such instruments as electron-microscopes are concerned, we again possess a number of checks. For just as there is continuity between what is seen through optical instruments and what is seen with the unaided vision, so there is continuity between what is seen through optical instruments and what is seen with the help of electron-microscopes. If, for example, we examine the structure of a living cell by means of an electron-microscope, we can easily check with an optical instrument that the picture given us is in general accurate. Of course, the electron-microscope provides us with a range of magnification beyond that of optical instruments, but given the continuity of what is revealed from the lowest magnification upwards, there is no reason to suppose that somewhere along the line, beyond the furthest point at which we can check, a radical form of distortion suddenly enters in.

To sum up on this point, there are good reasons for holding that scientific observation carried out with the help of instruments is as continuous with commonsense as that carried out with the senses alone. And, because of this, the use of instruments cannot form the basis of an argument in favour of cultural relativism.

2. Scientific claims concerning those things which are not and have not been observed, but which are nonetheless observable in principle

Claims of this kind are not very different from those of the first. There are no serious grounds for taking them to be culturally relative, since if and when clashes occur, there are public and accepted means of resolving them: appeals can be made at least in principle to observation, and observation — for the reasons already given — is a court of intercultural appeal.

The fact that disputes over claims of this kind may be settled only in principle does not argue in favour of cultural relativism, since, as was pointed out in Chapter 1, a claim can properly be said to be culturally relative only if there is no *sense* to saying that it is correct (or incorrect). But this is not the case here, as the following example will help to bring out. In the early eighteen-hundreds, the existence of a planet was argued for which would explain the odd behaviour of Uranus. At the time, naturally, the supposed planet was not observed, but nonetheless it was observable in principle; and because of this the assertion of its existence was decidedly not culturally relative. That is, from the outset it made perfectly good sense to say that the planet existed — or, for that matter, that it did not exist — since the observational method of dealing with the question was both well known and universally accepted by those who had given any thought to the matter. All this is borne out by the events of 1846, when the issue was settled without dispute or wrangle: the planet was observed, identified and given the name of Neptune. A similar example, already referred to, concerns what we call viruses. The existence of these was posited to explain the occurrence of certain diseases, and while they came to be observed only very much later, the assertion of their existence made perfectly adequate sense from the start.

The objection (already mentioned before) is sometimes made to this and related ways of arguing, that it assumes scientific observations to be describable independently of the theories which they are used to confirm or refute. But, the objection goes, scientific observations are necessarily theory-laden in such a way as to be describable only within the framework of their respective theories. Thus, in the examples given above, astronomers looked for a *planet*, biologists looked for *viruses:* both, in other words, sought to observe what could be described only within the terms of their pre-existing theories. How else indeed, it is asked, could their observations have served as appropriate tests for their theories?

Given the notion of the hierarchy of theory-ladenness described earlier, this objection may be met as follows. Planets and viruses, like all existing items, can be observed and recognised under more than one useful description — the description employed at any given moment depending on such things as immediate concerns and interests, or background theoretical beliefs. Because of this, it is possible to predict and look for observable occurrences capable of description equally within a high-level theory (for example, within Newton's theory of motion and gravity) and within theories at much lower levels, including that of commonsense. Further, and this is the crucial point, observations which come under descriptions low down on the scale of theory-ladenness can be, and often are, of considerable relevance in the testing of theories higher up. To illustrate the point at issue here, let us suppose that a Newtonian, relying on the content of his high-level theory, publicly predicts that 'a luminous body' will appear at such and such a time in such and such a quarter of the sky; or that a chemist tells us that if we mix the content of bottle A with that of bottle B we will see a flash and hear a bang. If in the outcome the Newtonian and the chemist prove to be wrong, their being so is undoubtedly relevant to the reliability or truth of their theories. Although it is more likely to be their auxiliary hypotheses which are at fault, not their theories, clearly it could be the latter.

A point worth adding is this. If observational occurrences which are to count as confirming or refuting could not effectively be described both within and without a given theory, men would rarely if ever be able to explain what they set out to explain. If astronomers, for example, could properly speak only of bodies having Newtonian mass, acceleration and so on, they would not be able to explain what first they set out to explain: namely, why it is that in the sky certain *luminous bodies wander about.*

To sum up on this issue, observations *can* be described and interpreted independently of the theories which they are employed to refute or confirm, and consequently scientific observations can continue to be employed as public, interculturally neutral tests of theories. Their acceptability and truth are not tied to, and therefore are not relative to, their theories in advance.

3. Scientific claims concerning what is not, has not been, and cannot even in principle be observed

Examples of this kind are claims about the existence and properties of such things as sub-atomic particles, absolute time and motion, curved space, action at a distance, fields of force. Different and sometimes sharply conflicting views have been held concerning these and items of their kind; and this, together with the fact that even in principle such conflicts cannot be settled by direct observation, has led scientists and philosophers at times to see the claims in question as of their essence neither true nor false. They have seen them instead as purely explanatory fictions or devices, bearing no literal descriptions at all.

The temptation to take this view is strongest at periods when theories long held almost to be self-evident are finally forced to give way to compelling rivals. However, the temptation should in general be resisted, on the grounds that the existence of rivals, the replacement of theories and the inability of direct observation to settle all disputes, do not of themselves constitute sufficient warrant for judging any given scientific claim to be a fiction. If they did, we would be forced to see most claims about the past, and many about the present, as mere fictional models. But there is no need to take this positivistic and counter-intuitive step since, as was argued in previous paragraphs, there are more ways than direct observation (even in principle) of settling disputes and appraising scientific truth-claims. We can appeal in addition to simplicity, range of explanation, lack of plausible alternatives, scope of prediction, ability to cope with anomalies, consonance with other beliefs and theories. Since we do all this at the level of commonsense, there is no reason why we should rule it out at the higher levels of science. *A fortiori* there is no reason why we should dismiss scientific claims as culturally relative simply on the grounds that they have replaced earlier rivals, are presently confronted with new ones, or cannot be settled by means of direct observation.

None of this of course is to suggest that science does not from time to time throw up difficult borderline cases. Clearly it does. There are instances in which it is not clear if a theory is intended to be literally descriptive, nor even if it could sensibly be intended as such. To illustrate the point, it was mentioned earlier that some philosophers and scientists find the notion of the curvature of space unintelligible when interpreted realistically, and that others feel the same about action at a distance or creation *ex nihilo*. In such cases it may well be the more reasonable course to interpret what is said as presenting the best models, or explanatory devices of whatever kind, that at present are available to us. But this is not at once to dismiss them as culturally relative, since what counts as best in the context may be what is judged by scientists interculturally to be best. In any event and as elsewhere in philosophy, borderline cases should not be allowed to force us into general conclusions.

There are borderline cases of another kind occurring in science, namely when on particular issues there is an equibalance of observational backing, explanatory power, and all the other criteria usually appealed to. But even in these extreme and rare circumstances we are not compelled to dismiss the competing claims as relative. For if at the moment we have no means of saying which of them has truth on its side, we are not forced to assert that it makes *no sense* to say that one of them has. On the contrary, it is perfectly plausible to assume that the issue will be rationally settled in the future, and that one of the contending claims will be judged to be true. Similar issues have after all been settled in the past.

To conclude on this chapter. There are no compelling grounds for treating the assertions and theories of science as culturally relative, not even when they concern such things as unobservable items. The reason for this is that when clashes occur men possess methods of judging which are continuous with those employed in commonsense, and which therefore are also intercultural.

This conclusion is reinforced by the fact that all attempts to make science a matter of culture have signally failed. This was the case with the Lysenko affair and with the Nazis' condemnation of supposedly Jewish science. By contrast, one of the more spectacular features of science is that it has been advanced and contributed to by men of widely different and often hostile cultures.

FURTHER READING

*Ayer, A.J. *Language, Truth and Logic*, London, 1936, Chap. 5.
*Barbour, I.G. *Issues in Science and Religion*, London, 1966, Chap. 6.
Bloor, D. "Popper's Mystification of Objective Knowledge", *Science Studies*, 4 (1974), pp. 65-76.
Bloor, D. *Knowledge and Social Imagery*, London, 1976.
*Chalmers, A.F. *What is this Thing called Science?*, Queensland, 1976.
Churchland, P.M. *Scientific Realism and the Plasticity of Mind*, Cambridge, 1979.
Cohen, M.R. *Reason and Nature*, New York, 1931.
Esposito, J.L. "Science and Conceptual Relativism", *Philosophical Studies*, 31 (1977), pp. 269-277.
Feigl, H. & Brodbeck, May. *Readings in the Philosophy of Science*, New York, 1953.
Feyerabend, P.K. "Science Without Experience", *Journal of Philosophy*, 66 (1969), pp. 791-4.
Frank, P. *Philosophy of Science*, Englewood Cliffs, N.J., 1957.
Gale, G. *Theory of Science*, New York, 1979.
*Gregory, R.L. *Eye and Brain,* London, 1972.
Hanson, N.R. *Patterns of Discovery*, Cambridge, 1958.
*Harré, R. *An Introduction to the Logic of the Sciences,* London, 1960.
Harré, R. *The Principles of Scientific Thinking*, London, 1970.
*Harré, R. *The Philosophies of Science: An Introductory Survey*, Oxford, 1972.
Harré, R. *Problems of Scientific Revolution*, Oxford, 1975.
*Hempel, C.G., *Philosophy of Natural Science*, Englewood Cliffs, N.J., 1966.
Hesse, M. "Duhem, Quine and a New Empiricism", *Knowledge and Necessity* (Royal Institute of Philosophy Lectures, vol. 3), London, 1970.
Horton, R. "African Traditional Thought andWestern Science", *Rationality*, Wilson, B. (ed.), Blackwell, Oxford, 1970.
*Körner, S. *What is Philosophy?*, London, 1969, Chap. 5.
Kuhn, T.S. *The Structure of Scientific Revolutions*, Chicago & London, 1962.
Lakatos, I. & Musgrave, A. *Criticism and the Growth of Knowledge,* Cambridge, 1970.
Laudan, L. *Progress and its Problems,* London, 1977.
*Magee, B. *Popper,* London, 1975.
Medawar, P. *Induction and Intuition in Scientific Thought,* London, 1969.
*Morick, H. *Challenges to Empiricism,* Belmont, California, 1972, Introduction, The Critique of Contemporary Empiricism.
*Nagel, E. *The Structure of Science,* London, 1961.
Nidditch, P.H. *The Philosophy of Science* (Oxford Readings), Oxford, 1968.
*Oatley, K. *Brain Mechanisms and Mind,* London, 1972.
Pap, A. *Introduction to the Philosophy of Science,* Glencoe, Ill., 1962.
*Popper, K. *Conjectures and Refutations*, London, 1963, Chap. 1.
*Popper, K. *Unended Quest*, London, 1976.
*Quinton, A. *The Nature of Things*, London, 1973, Chap. 10.
Scheffler, I. *Science and Subjectivity,* Indianapolis, 1967.
Smart, J.J.C. *Philosophy and Scientific Realism*, London, 1963.
*Warnock, M. *Schools of Thought,* Faber & Faber, London, 1977.
Wartofsky, M.W. *Conceptual Foundations of Scientific Thought,* New York, 1968.

CHAPTER 3
CULTURAL RELATIVISM AND THE SOCIAL SCIENCES

Attention was drawn in the Introduction to the number of influential sociologists of education and perhaps others who hold that all knowledge is socially constructed and relative to this or that culture. But on the grounds that it is difficult to say what precisely these writers have in mind and even more difficult to follow their arguments, I suggested that the simplest procedure would be to examine the main areas of what is usually taken to be knowledge, and to show what at any rate could *not* sensibly be asserted concerning them. In Chapter 1 accordingly I went on to examine what I referred to as men's *commonsense* beliefs and principles, and in Chapter 2 I turned to the natural sciences, arguing that in each case the knowledge concerned is not culturally relative, nor in any non-trivial sense socially constructed. In this chapter I will argue for the same sort of thesis in relation to the social sciences, taking the latter to be those areas of investigation and knowledge which pertain to men as beings with intentions, meanings and social interactions — areas therefore which include psychology, sociology, economics, anthropology, (much of) history and political science.

In several respects the social sciences are even more difficult to treat of than the natural. To begin with, there is no agreement even among their practitioners about what they do or should do, nor is it possible to point to an acknowledged group of successful social scientists in the way that it is possible to point to a group of successful natural scientists. Whatever Galileo, Newton, Einstein and others may be thought precisely to have accomplished, it is at least agreed that they were highly successful. There is no such agreement about who have been successful in the social sciences, nor indeed is it even agreed that *any* have. Some leaders in the field hold that we are in early days yet and that the social sciences await their Kepler or Galileo to get things going.[1] By contrast, others argue that what is needed is not the advent of a sociological Kepler or Galileo, but the realisation that the social sciences are fundamentally different from the natural sciences, and that attempts to imitate them are seriously mistaken.[2]

Further difficulties arise from the fact that there exist several schools of social scientists with quite opposing aims, methods and practices. There are, for example, positivists, empirical theorists, phenomenologists, interpretivists, Marxists and critical theorists.[3] To add to the complexity, while some of the differences among these are due to deep-seated metaphysical and ideological commitments, others appear to be due simply to mis-understandings. For example, as will be argued later, many of those who are hostile to the view that the social and natural sciences are alike, are hostile to it because they have in mind a narrow and mistaken idea of what the natural sciences are in the first place. Finally, more than occasionally the writings of social scientists are unintelligible, not only to laymen and workers in other fields, but to their closest colleagues.[4]

To take account of these many difficulties and to go through all of the rival views on the nature of the social sciences would be considerably beyond the scope of this book. What I intend therefore is the following. I will begin by outlining and defending what seems to me the most acceptable view on the nature of the social sciences, and I will try to show that if this view is correct the claims and theories of the latter cannot with plausibility be thought of as culturally relative. After that I will turn to the principal objections to the view in question, and argue that these objections can be met, and further that even if they could not, the findings of the social sciences would still not be shown to be relative.

The nature of the social sciences in general

The view here to be defended is that while the object of enquiry proper to the social sciences — namely, men as sentient, intelligent and social beings — is different from that of the natural sciences, the two are fundamentally the same in their methods, aims and purposes.

It will be recalled that in the last chapter I argued that when the natural scientist investigates the world, he does so with a mind which is far from empty; on the contrary, I claimed, it contains a wide range of principles, beliefs, memories and attitudes. It contains, for example, commonsense beliefs and memories; beliefs and principles relating to values; principles of logic; metaphysical principles and beliefs; principles of economy, simplicity and elegance; already accepted scientific theories, hunches and half-form-ulated opinions. Because of this, when he examines, observes, experiments, or weighs up a new theory, the natural scientist cannot know in advance what considerations in particular will prevail. There is no single and simple criterion that he can turn to. If, for example, he accepts a theory, he may do so for one or more of many reasons, ranging from its immediate fit with obser-vational findings to its comparative simplicity or its power in bringing other theories into unity. At the same time and for similar reasons he does not always have the same end in view. Sometimes he aims at amassing descriptive detail; sometimes at establishing correlations; sometimes at coming up with new explanations; sometimes at discovering what onto-logical items lie behind this or that set of appearances; sometimes at modifying a theory or at getting it to accord with others.

To bring out in some detail this complexity in the nature of the natural sciences, two sets of points were drawn up in Chapter 2: the first serving principally as a series of reminders about what the natural sciences are not, the second attempting more positively to say what they are (and do). In the following sections these same two sets of points will be employed to bring out the nature of the social sciences, and to show how akin these are to their natural counterparts.

Some negative points concerning the social sciences

The social sciences are not simply accumulations of observed facts, nor do they consist of generalisations naively drawn from the latter. Theories and explanations such as those in terms of suppressed inflation, false consciousness, perfectly free markets, latent functions or super-egos, clearly go beyond what is or may be observed, and cannot be reduced to statements or generalisations about the latter.

The claims, hypotheses and theories of the social sciences do not any more than those of the natural sciences or of commonsense result from a direct confrontation of the senses with reality. When we perceive the social world, as when we perceive the natural world, interpretation takes place, so that identical sets of physiological data registered by the senses of two or more persons may be interpreted in substantially different ways. Thus what a psychologist trained in Piaget's cognitive theories sees in a classroom, just as what the trained biologist sees under the microscope, is very different from what the rest of us see.

Observation is not the only important element in the formation, acceptance or rejection of theories in the social sciences. For example, simplicity and scope of explanation are often considered of equal if not greater importance; as they are, say, in Marxist theories of economics or Freudian theories of psychoanalysis. Indeed it is noticeable that many social scientists do no observing at all over long periods of time (or at any rate no more than the rest of us), but spend their energies – not improperly – in attempting to work out satisfying theories in terms of alienation, stratification, false consciousness or whatever.

No given amount of evidence purporting either to confirm or refute an hypothesis is to be taken as decisive. It is always possible that the supposed confirming or refuting evidence will itself shortly be set aside as unsatisfactory, or that means will be found of explaining it away and allowing the hypothesis in question to be continued with (or persistently rejected). Thus no given amount of evidence is decisively for (or against) the hypothesis that social isolation increases the probability of early death or suicide, or for the view that education is a major influence for social change.

Hypotheses and theories are not to be thought of as confirmed or refuted severally, in isolation. For example, the hypothesis has occasionally been put forward that a person's level of intelligence is to be explained in terms of genetic factors rather than environment. Such an hypothesis cannot be put to the test by itself, for it assumes the truth of others. It assumes, for example, that there exist adequate means of judging intelligence; that the language used in tests is free from cultural bias; that hidden and unsuspected environmental factors are not really responsible for the apparent differences in intelligence anyway. And so on. Thus if, when we set about evaluating this hypothesis, the evidence from our tests appears strongly to support it, we are not justified in claiming it to be true unless we can with equal justification assert that the background hypotheses also are true. If, say, we are not sure of the adequacy of our tests, or have not seriously looked at the evidence for rival theories, our acceptance of the main hypothesis is unwarranted. And similar remarks apply to the *refutation* of hypotheses or theories. Acceptance of a refutation is only warranted if confidence in our background beliefs and assumptions is equally warranted.

No conclusions arrived at in the social sciences are incorrigible: like the natural sciences, they are not systems in which the conclusions are entailed by their premisses. To revert to the example given above, however strongly our present evidence may appear to favour the conclusion that intelligence is (or is not) genetically determined, that evidence cannot guarantee the conclusion, and indeed is logically compatible with its contradictory. The social scientist then has to bear in mind that all conclusions, however well supported, are open in principle to correction, revision and even downright substitution.

There is no single kind of explanation in the social sciences which can properly serve as a model for all. To begin with, some explanations are appeals to established regularities: as when, following Durkheim, social scientists explain the frequency of suicide in a particular group by appealing to a regularity occurring between suicides and low levels of social cohesion; or when they explain the educational success of a given pupil by appealing to his family background and class. Other explanations do not appeal to mere regularities and correlations, but to *causes*: as when it is said that the rapid growth of sociology causes attacks on it by those who fear its social consequences or its academic competition;[5] or when it is argued with Keynes that the cause of unemployment is inadequate aggregate demand. Still other explanations appeal to functions: as when it is argued (again with Durkheim) that the function of religion is the expression and reinforcement of social solidarity; or when more widely it is argued that the function of social structures is the satisfying of basic human needs. Yet further explanations appeal to the existence, or supposed existence, of unobserved and sometimes even unobservable items. Thus economists refer in their explanations to such things as economic man, suppressed inflation, free market forces and deficit government spendings; historians speak of the spirit or temper of this or that age; sociologists of ideal types, role distances and latent functions; psychologists of the subconscious, faculties and basic needs; and so on. Finally, many explanations in the social sciences consist in locating what is to be explained within a framework of human beliefs, rules, attitudes and conventions. We explain, for example, the banking system in this way, or the use by Catholics of incense in their ceremonies, or such practices as games of football and cricket. None of these can be explained adequately by appeals to observed correlations, causal links or functions: a grasp of people's beliefs, intentions, meanings and the rest seem to be at least equally essential.

It is obvious that the progress of the social sciences is not rectilinear, since not only are theories endlessly rejected and replaced,[6] but entire methods and lines of enquiry are abandoned. Further, as was pointed out earlier, it is not even agreed among their own practitioners that the social sciences have in any serious way yet properly begun, let alone made significant progress. As Poincaré acidly remarked of sociology, it is 'the science with the most methods and the fewest results'.

Finally, as in the case of the natural sciences, there are no known rules, and probably could be none, enabling social scientists to arrive at theories mechanically. It takes what we refer to as genius, together with a good measure of luck, to come up with theories like those of economic man or the unconscious, to grasp the significance of economic factors in the course of history, or to focus on and take seriously the relation between unemployment and the level of aggregate demand. We do not even know what is the most suitable environment (if indeed there is such a thing) for the producing of this creative activity and genius. We simply live in hope.

Positive remarks on the nature of the social sciences

The social sciences, like the natural, are in many if not most areas plainly descriptive. The anthropologist, the sociologist, the historian and the rest are all interested in finding out what societies, cultures, belief systems, institutions and so on are like, and while they seek also to do such things as give explanations and make predictions, this does not mean to say that their descriptions are not central to their task or that they are of comparatively small importance. In any case, the regularities and correlations which they establish may themselves properly be seen as constituting no more than descriptions of social reality. On the other hand, not all propositions of the social sciences are to be construed as descriptions – not even when they are couched in descriptive language and were originally intended to give information in a straightforward and literal sense. For example, reference to the subconscious, to suppressed desires or to roles is best understood as a reference to imagined items introduced as a means of helping us to understand occurrences which themselves can be described literally. We are not really in possession of a subconscious or suppressed desires, existing as distinct ontological items, but it may help to imagine that we are; nor are we

41

really actors on a stage, merely playing at being such things as unwilling schoolboys, soldiers or lovers.

While observation is not the only element in the procedures of the social sciences, it is of central importance to them. The social scientist, not only when giving accurate descriptions or making predictions but also when putting forward explanations, will be more convincing if he has observational backing to his claims.[7] To take examples, if he appeals to a correlation between income and level of educational attainment, to a causal link between wage-claims and inflation, to this or that interpretation of what the Nuer mean by saying that twins are birds, or to the existence of latent functions — in all such cases his appeals will be considerably more plausible if he has observational evidence in their favour. In the case of the appeal to a correlation between income and level of educational attainment, his claim will be greatly strengthened if, say, other investigators come up with the same findings; or in the case of the belief that twins are birds, if the Nuer are observed to behave accordingly.[8]

This leads to the general point that while, because of the nature of non-deductive reasoning, observational evidence cannot guarantee the truth or falsity of theories or hypotheses, it is typically of considerable value in supporting or refuting them. Piaget's theories, for example, were certainly supported (*not* rendered certain) by the evidence of his countless experiments, and Marx's theory, at least if not merely qualified, was refuted by the fact that Communism took root in Russia rather than in advanced industrial societies.

As is the case with the natural sciences, all observation made use of in the social sciences is theory-laden. For the reasons which were given in Chapter 2 however, this does not mean that observations can never be separated out from the theories which they are held to support. It was argued, for example, that when the astronomer talks of planets, or the biologist of viruses, the observational statements made by them can be expressed in language perfectly well understood by persons who do not share their theoretical views or indeed are totally ignorant of them. The same is true in the social sciences. Many of the observational findings appealed to by Piaget, Freud or Keynes, in order to support their theories, could have been described in language intelligible to those who were not even aware of such theories. What is more, if once Piaget, Freud and Keynes had formulated their theories, their observations were from that time on *entirely* coloured by those theories, the latter would not have been able to explain the observational occurrences which were the cause of puzzlement in the first place. Freud, for example, set out to explain certain sorts of behaviour. But if after formulating his theory the patterns of behaviour which he appealed to for confirmation could only be apprehended by him in terms of the theory itself, clearly he could not have explained what he set out to make sense of from the start. For, like any other theory, Freud's was meant precisely to explain data as apprehended in terms not forming part of the subsequent theory. This point will be returned to briefly later.

If the question is asked, What is the aim of the social sciences?, there is no single answer to be given, as there was no single answer in the case of the natural sciences. Sometimes the aim is detailed description; sometimes generalisation; sometimes explanation; sometimes prediction and utility; sometimes the resolution of metaphysical or conceptual problems.[9]

The doctrine of cultural relativism and the social sciences

It will be argued later that, given the nature of the social sciences as outlined above, there is no greater reason for considering their claims to be culturally relative than there was for so considering the claims of the natural sciences. However, there is at least a *prima facie* case in favour of the doctrine of cultural relativism in what touches the social sciences, and it deserves to be looked at. It is a case which is rarely if ever spelled out in detail, but it is widely supported and is reflected in remarks which are heard almost daily, even in academic circles.

It is said, for example, that all history is contemporary history: meaning that when historians attempt to enquire into, assess or explain periods other than their own, they are unable to do so except in terms of their own values, principles, categories, institutions and the like; and that because of this what they say is merely and necessarily a projection of their own minds and thoughts.

It is said — sometimes it would seem by anthropologists themselves[10] — that the values and institutions of all cultures are self-validating, that no culture can be said to be superior to another, and even that cultures are unintelligible except to those who are inside them and share in their forms of life. From this it follows that what the anthropologist and his or her fellow-workers have to say is culturally relative. For if they succeed in getting on the inside of the culture which they are studying, their claims and conclusions will be relative to that culture: if they do not succeed, what they say will be relative to whatever culture they *are* on the inside of.

It is said that all translators are inescapably locked within their own mental structures, and that consequently renderings of, say, Homer, Plato or Kant are able to tell you more of the translators' minds than ever they can of the original authors'.

It is said that (thanks to their social conditioning) economists, political scientists and social commentators of all kinds are biased in such a way that in areas of dispute their conclusions are beyond arbitration: consciously or unconsciously they pick out and will take seriously only those pieces of evidence which serve to bolster their preconceived opinions and persuasions. We can quickly check this, it is added, by listening to any discussion or debate between scholars, politicians or laymen coming from one ideological background and their counterparts from another.

It is said by 'radical' educationists that *everything* which passes as knowledge in schools is relative to those who have power over the curriculum: that the history, economics, politics, human geography and the rest of the things that are taught are relative to the classes or whatever other sub-groups teachers and administrators happen to belong to.

Many other comments of a like nature are made both in popular conversation and (though usually as asides) in scholarly discourse, and it will be useful now to spell out rather more fully and examine the arguments which appear to lie behind them.

The social sciences and classification

The first argument used to support the cultural relativism of the social sciences begins by noting that one of the more fundamental tasks of social scientists is *classification*: sociologists, for example, are fundamentally concerned to classify in terms of such things as institutions, roles or primary and secondary groups. But, the argument continues, categories or divisions of these kinds are not 'given'; on the contrary, they are elements in conceptual schemes which have been created and imposed by this or that group of men. Because of this, it is said, they do not match up with what is already there in the world. Rather they reflect back the interests and mental activities of the cultures within which they take their rise and within which subsequently they are employed. From this it is further held that they and the propositions in which they occur are correspondingly relative.

This argument is not persuasive if and when it is intended (as often it is) to apply to *all* of the classifications employed, and to all of the propositions asserted in the social sciences. To begin with, it does not follow from the fact that this or that classification is not 'given' that the propositions making use of it are true only relatively. Surely not every assertion is like the statement that the left (or right) side of the road is the correct one to drive on. To illustrate this, let us suppose that some cultures do not have the concept of 'circular'. It does not follow from this that the assertion that the coins in my pocket are circular is true relative to my culture but not to theirs. On the contrary it would seem to be a matter of plain fact, *something to be discovered*; though obviously not something to be discovered by those without the relevant concepts. In the same way, many if not most of the propositions asserted in the social sciences are statements concerning matters of fact and discovery. For example, it is a matter of fact and discovery that in certain societies only some people own the means of production, and that those who do own them are able to exercise more influence and power than those who do not. There are of course difficulties in spelling out what is meant by the means of production, and what is meant by influence and power. But what-

44

ever these difficulties, the conceptual distinctions are at any rate clear enough to let us recognise on the one hand, say, a wealthy owner of industrial plant, and on the other hand an unpropertied, unskilled labourer. In this particular case no doubt it may properly be said that the relevant conceptual divisions are peculiar to some societies. But it may not be said in addition that the matters of fact involved are peculiar. On the contrary, they are open to verification by all men, provided only that (as a matter of trivial truth) all men are in possession of the needed concepts. There are other cases, however, where not only the propositions asserted are matters of fact and discovery, but where so too are the classifications which those propositions make use of in the first place. To take an example from what is of pretty obvious concern to the social sciences, the classifications of people into parents and children, aunts and uncles and the rest, are the results of plain discovery of fact. If men in any groups or societies are without the concepts applying here, it can only be because they have failed to notice, or perhaps have not been interested in noticing, the relevant facts. But facts they are for all that.

In short, there is no justification for dismissing the social sciences as culturally relative on the grounds that they make use of (their own or more common) classifications. It is worth adding that on this point the natural sciences are no different. For the natural scientist also employs an understructure of classifications. Yet, if the arguments of Chapter 2 were sound, this does not entail that whatever true propositions a given natural scientist asserts are true only relative to his and kindred cultures. For example, if a physicist speaks of such things as atoms, protons and electrons, it cannot plausibly be held that what he has to say is a matter of truth relative to his and like cultures, but not to others. It is not true, for example, only here or there that the atoms of the element iron contain twenty-six protons, nor has this become true only in the twentieth century. If men in some societies and at some periods do not hold to the proposition that the atomic number of iron is twenty-six, this is not because that proposition is true only at some times and in some societies, but because the men in question do not possess the conceptual or others means of grasping what is being said. When they do come to acquire what is needed, they also reach a position of finding out for themselves what is open in principle to the discovery of all men.

A general point to be noticed here (and taken up again later) is that those who do hold the social sciences to be culturally relative, and in addition are prepared to argue for their case, usually attempt to do so on empirical grounds. But let us ask: What empirical evidence could count here? It would have to be of a sort to show that, as a matter of reasonably common occurrence, even when people in different cultures understand and grasp the grounds for what is asserted by others, they nonetheless reach different conclusions and do so perseveringly — after genuine and strenuous efforts to reach a common conclusion. To take an example, it is sometimes asserted at any rate by Western social scientists that fewer people living in cities go to church than those living in country areas. Let us now suppose that social scientists in China or Japan deny this, and further that upon enquiry we find that they and their Western opposites are talking about the same cities and country areas; that both seem to understand the same things by 'people' and 'church'; that neither party has an obvious vested interest in the assertion at issue (or in its denial); that both have made every effort to find out and explain why they disagree. And so on. In circumstances of this kind we would indeed have good *prima facie* grounds for suspecting that the claims of the social sciences are culturally relative, if not altogether worse. But of course no such circumstances have (at any rate regularly) been recorded.

The social sciences and selectivity

The argument for cultural relativism in the social sciences that will now be looked at is closely related to the first, and it comes to the following. When a social scientist studies any period, culture or group, it follows from there being in each of these a limitless number of features that could be focused upon, that the social scientist in question has to make a selection. Therefore, what comes to be looked at, recorded or interpreted is again not 'given' but is 'chosen', and consequently reflects the interest of, and is relative to, its chooser. For example, when a social historian (to count him as a social scientist) sets out to write an account of Europe in the nineteenth century, he is confronted with what in practice is a boundless mass of material. What events, then, or even kinds of events, situations and the like is he to pick out? What persons is he to focus upon? What speeches or conversations is he to record? There is no answer, it is urged, to be found in the nature of things; and the historian himself must choose. But because of this and because different historians make different choices, historical accounts themselves turn out to be different, and these differences can only be explained as reflections of the dissimilar interests, appraisals and value-judgments of the historians or perhaps of the cultures within which they are nurtured. And the same sort of thing is true of anthropologists, sociologists, psychologists and other social scientists. Strongly influenced by their own commitments and by the cultures or parties to which they belong, they exercise *choice* in what they will look at, examine and explain.

This argument again is not convincing. From the fact that the social scientist is obliged to select it does not follow that the truth of his claims and the validity of his explanations are relative to his culture or personal views. For surely there are common human interests which set at least some limits to his choices. To illustrate this with some extreme but relevant examples, it is implausible to suggest that an anthropologist's range of choice is so open that in studying a society he is at liberty to ignore such things as plagues, wars and migrations, and to concentrate on the colour of people's hair or the number of windows which they choose to put in their huts. What counts as important to a man, whether anthropologist or not, depends not only on his culture but on his nature; and for this reason pestilence, fire and sword will always be of more significance to him than such things as fashions in building. Further, even if we allow for the sake of argument that the social scientist does have total liberty to choose, it does not follow that what finally he decides upon to record and explain are not matters of common fact and discovery. When the sociologist records that the decline in church attendance over the last sixty years has been greater in European countries than in the United States, his claim is no more culturally relative than that of the historian who records that the German army invaded Russia in June 1941, and was halted at Stalingrad by troops under the command of Marshall Zhukov. So, in cases of these kinds, social scientists can be accused at the very worst of producing partial accounts; and even that of course need not be the end of the story. For partial accounts can be criticised, filled out and balanced up. Social scientists from different cultures can get together, and with the help above all of those who have no obvious and special interest in what conclusions are reached, they stand a reasonable chance of coming to agreement. There is no reason in principle why questions in the social sciences should not be settled in this way, as often enough they have been in the natural sciences — from the time of Galileo to that of Lysenko and beyond.

The social sciences and values

The third argument for the cultural relativism of the social sciences rests on the double claim that they essentially involve the making of value judgments, and that value judgments in turn are always culturally relative. Sometimes it is added that not only do the social sciences as a matter of fact necessarily involve the making of value judgments, but that morally they ought to: that the social scientist fails in his duty who does not speak out against the discriminations, oppressions and deprivations which he discovers in this or that society. If, like all value judgments, moral judgments are relative, then the social scientist along with other men of good faith must boldly commit himself. Morality is a matter not of truth but of commitment.

Against this last view it will be argued in Chapter 4 that morality is in fact a matter of truth, and that because of this the social scientist is able to make rationally defensible moral judgments about the affairs of the societies or groups which he studies. But it does not follow from this that when he makes his moral judgments he makes them *qua* social scientist. In fact he does not. For, as will now be argued, the social sciences are not in any peculiar way value-laden.

There are several ways in which statements and judgments can be value-laden. They can be value-laden because the concepts which they employ are contextually evaluations (if, for example, people are referred to as 'niggers')

47

or simply because they rather than others are singled out for mention (as happens, say, when true but prejudiced evidence is given in courts of law). Perhaps in a weak sense all statements may be said to be value-laden, on the grounds that their being stated at all shows that at least somebody attaches importance to them. Again statements may be said to be value-laden because the concepts they use are the results of prior classifications which themselves are evidence of evaluation. These and like cases are examples of covert value-ladenness. But of course there are plenty of overt, straightforward value-judgments too, and as many again that lie somewhere between. However, whatever the type of value-ladenness or value judgment involved, the same question is to be asked: Can the social scientist avoid bringing to his professional utterances the values of the society, culture or sub-culture to which he belongs?

The first point to be made in attempting to answer this question is that there does clearly seem to be a firm distinction between statements of fact and judgments of value. For example, when the social scientist tells us that divorce rates are higher in large cities than in small towns, he is making an utterance of a very different kind from that made by the preacher who tells us that divorce is a corrupting and evil thing. And there is a similar difference to be found between the statement that King John signed Magna Charta in 1215 and the claim that he was among the most vicious and wanton kings to wear the English crown. The difference between the sorts of utterance here is plain enough, even if it is argued that concepts like that of 'divorce' or 'king' are the outcome of prior processes of classification, or that to mention divorce rates and regal activities is already to show what is judged to be important — important enough at least to investigate and record. However, it was shown a little while ago that neither classification nor selection is able of itself to turn matters of common fact into matters of cultural relativity. Further, even in cases where statements have to deal with such things as discrimination, oppression, racial prejudice or class hatred, the social scientist can still stay on the side of facts by spelling out extensionally what he means by these things, or by providing us with paradigms. He does not have to *condemn* racial intolerance (or whatever) when he records or explains its occurrence. For all that concerns him as a social scientist, he may thoroughly approve of it or he may be totally indifferent to it.

None of this, however, will satisfy some philosophers and social scientists. All men, these will insist, have their prejudices; all men are biased. All of us, they will continue, tend to see what we want to see; to notice favourable but not unfavourable evidence; to attribute evil intentions to those whom we dislike; to trust and believe those whose judgments are on our side; to look for and find explanations which will justify our conduct. And so on. In short, we see neither facts nor persons as they are, but view them in the light of our interests, hopes, expectations and the like, or in the light of those of our country, race, class or some other group.

48

Views of this kind may serve to remind us that social scientists run all the risks of other men in being open to partiality and bias; but they do nothing to show that the effects of these cannot be avoided. By contrast, there are at least two good reasons for believing that they can.

First, men can be brought to an awareness of their prejudices, and strive to overcome them. What is more, there is evidence — enough to satisfy all but the sceptic — that sometimes they succeed. Only the sceptic will deny, for example, that the scholar who is aware of his religious, national or other prejudices can make allowances for them in carrying out his inquiries and weighing the evidence presented to him. Second, clearly not all scholars share the *same* prejudices, and on most if not all issues at least some of them will be neutral. For this reason it is (in principle) possible for them to work together, correcting and counterbalancing one another's views where necessary, and drawing attention to their disagreements when these are not resolved. For example, if two sets of writings, one by a Marxist and another by a Catholic, contain a conflict of opinion over a supposed series of events, it is possible for the writers themselves or for a third party to take account of the background differences of commitment involved, and in the light of these to make an accurate re-assessment. It may of course be objected that this sort of thing does not happen very often; but the issue here is not one of the frequency of the occurrence but of its possibility.

It may be worth adding, as elsewhere, that if someone wishes to persevere with the claim that it is *not* possible to take an unprejudiced view in describing and explaining human actions, it is incumbent upon him to produce evidence to support his claim. Further, he will need to show that what evidence he does produce is itself not prejudiced. If it is, there is no reason why we should accept it.

The social sciences and theory-ladenness

If the investigations and consequent statements of the social sciences are often said to be essentially value-laden, they are also said to be theory-laden; and from this it is argued that they must be culturally relative, on the grounds that theories are paradigmatically cultural creations.

This notion of theory-ladenness has already been explained and mentioned more than once before, and need now be recalled only in summary form. To say that statements are theory-laden is to say that they are neither true nor verifiable independently of the theory or theories within which they are embedded. Or, to put this more broadly, it is to say that statements cannot be true in isolation, but only in conjunction with an already existing set of beliefs and assumptions. Just as what we see is fashioned and structured in accordance with the present state of our retina and central nervous system, so what we take to be true is fashioned and structured according to the state of our existing beliefs.

To this argument it may be said that even if all statements are in some sense and at some level theory-laden, little follows that can favour the cultural relativist. To begin with, there are plenty of discoveries and corresponding statements which cannot with *any* plausibility be thought of as merely culturally relative. For example, it was believed for centuries that bees were generated from rotting carcasses, that the function of the lungs was to cool the heart, that the blood's motion in the body was one of ebb and flow. By contrast, we now believe that bees are reproduced sexually, that the heart acts as a pump, and that the blood circulates in the body. Could we seriously hold that these present-day beliefs are not true in a way that their earlier rivals never were? Could we, that is, hold that no more is to be said of them than that they are embedded in theories of a different period and different culture? Surely not. For surely any culture which holds that bees are generated spontaneously, or anything of the kind, holds what is false *simpliciter*. And similar examples abound in statements concerning societies and cultures themselves. It used to be thought that Britain before the invasion of the Romans was inhabited by tribes of people without developed trade, crafts or coinage. We now know that this is false, and it makes little sense to add that it was nonetheless true to or for the people who believed it. It is better to say outright that at the time of believing it those people were simply wrong.

It is not just that because of counter-examples like these it is *intuitively* implausible to suppose that statements in being theory-laden are culturally relative. It is rather that (for reasons already canvassed more than once) there *could* be no rational grounds for holding to such a view. We *have* to share in a core of common beliefs with others before we can even begin to establish in what beliefs these others differ. And as long as there exists this common core of beliefs, there also exists (for that very reason) a limit on the scope of the first premiss in the basic argument for cultural relativism. For that premiss, it will be recalled, relies exclusively on the existence of cultural differences. In brief, *whether or not all statements are theory-laden, they are not all culturally relative.*

Another point worth mentioning is that it does not follow from the fact, if it is a fact, that theories are cultural creations, that their truth is only culturally relative. The origins of theories should not be confused with what they are about, nor with their justification. Thus the claim that human beings are descended from other species cannot seriously be thought to be true only within the culture which gave birth to the theory of evolution. Rather, reality is such that if this theory is true at all it is true without reference to any culture or cultures (to the exclusion of others).

Finally, a point which is often made but not always taken seriously is that if all statements in being theory-laden are culturally relative, there are no good grounds for excluding the claim itself that all statements are relative. And a kindred consequence is that since the utterances of the social sciences would now turn out to be culturally relative, they would have no greater right to be heard (except within their own cultures) than, say, the oracle of Delphi. This point is in no way a conclusive refutation of cultural relativism, but even so it deserves better than to be ignored.

Are any of the claims of the social sciences culturally relative?

Now that the principal arguments in favour of the cultural relativity of social-scientific claims have been looked at, we can turn to showing more directly, and in the light of the analysis which was presented earlier on in this chapter, that the social sciences are not culturally relative.

When the natural sciences were under discussion, a distinction was drawn between those statements which concern the directly or indirectly observable, and those which concern what even in principle is unobservable. In treating now of the social sciences a distinction may be drawn which is roughly parallel to this but which avoids essential reference to observation (in deference to those who dislike talk of 'observing' human actions).

This parallel distinction is between statements immediately continuous with 'commonsense' (as understood in Chapter 2), and statements well removed from it.

Social-scientific statements immediately continuous with commonsense

For a set of beings to count as men, to be capable of what we call 'human actions', they must possess in common with their fellow beings a number of basic properties and abilities, among which are the following: the ability to reason inductively and deductively; the ability to understand and use language; the ability to interact intelligently with others (whether by language or otherwise); the ability to recognise a set of referents and properties singled out by all men;[11] the use of a number of common metaphysical assumptions. (Examples of the latter are that material objects in some sense or other continue to exist when unperceived, and that the world will continue to behave with a tolerable measure of orderliness and stability.) All of this has been argued for already, and it has been argued too that it is because and only because men share these properties and abilities – in a word because there is an area of 'commonsense' in which all men participate – that they are able at all to come under the scrutiny and investigation of the social sciences.

It was argued further that in the natural sciences there is one level of activity which is simply a systematic extension of the activities of common-sense; that when Mendel, for example, observed and reasoned inductively about his peas, he was doing in a more sophisticated fashion only what the native hunter is doing when he observes and reasons about the fish in his stream or about the predictable behaviour of currents of water. But much the same applies to the social sciences. For it can be argued that these contain a precisely corresponding level of activity: namely, an immediate extension of what all men, however 'primitive', engage in when they take note of and reason inductively about the *actions of their fellow men*. Certainly all men do engage in these kinds of activity, and indeed must do if they are to merit being called men at all. For to be unable to reason about one's fellow men would be to be unable to make intelligent predictions of any kind about their behaviour, and therefore to be unable to interact intelligently with them or even to learn and speak their language. All men are able to do these things on pain of not being men at all, or of being men in no more than outward form.

It follows from this that the social scientist is in much the same position as his counterpart in the natural sciences when at this first level he makes use of his powers of perceiving and reasoning in order to describe, explain and generalise upon the facts before him — that is, when he acts as a methodical, systematic and persevering man of commonsense. And (again like the natural scientist) he is not engaged here in an undertaking which is only culturally relative. For given that the activities of commonsense cannot in any way be culturally relative — since together they make up that common core of abilities which are *constitutive of human activity* — there is every reason to accept that the kind of immediate extension of those activities which is now under consideration is not culturally relative either.

There is a second argument which can be used to show that the activities and claims of the social sciences at the level now being discussed are not culturally relative. It relies on the point made several times in earlier chapters, that the truth of a claim may properly be thought of as relative to a culture only on the following conditions. There must exist a rival claim or claims in some other culture or cultures. There must be no means of discovering which of the rivals, if any, is uniquely correct. It must not even make sense to say that one of the rivals is uniquely correct.

In the case of those social-scientific claims which are now being considered, neither of these last two conditions is fulfilled, as may be illustrated in the following example. If a social scientist in one culture asserts, while another in another culture denies, that the suicide rate is higher in Sweden than in Ireland, or higher among the unemployed than among those at work, we know perfectly well how the issue is to be settled (at any rate in theory). The two parties will have to make sure that they are talking about the same things; they will have to re-check their figures; they will have to do further research; and so on. And because we know this, we clearly have no grounds for suggesting that it does not even make sense to say that one of the rival claims is correct to the exclusion of the other.

Social-scientific statements well removed from commonsense

Statements in the social sciences which cannot properly be classified as belonging to the area of commonsense are entirely on a par with those in the natural sciences which also are well removed from it. For this reason it will be useful to recall in the following outline what was said concerning the latter.

The natural sciences from period to period refer to the existence of things altogether beyond the scope of observation and commonsense. They refer to such things as: electrons; the mean free path between atoms or molecules; motion totally unaffected by forces; frictionless surfaces; vital forces; action at a distance; absolute space and time. For the most part there is no great disagreement at present concerning the ontological status of these; some of them have been universally accepted as real; some have been accepted as unreal but nonetheless useful; some have been universally, or almost universally, rejected as neither real nor useful. But there are other cases, as there have been in the past, where there are serious divisions of opinion.

When divisions of opinion of this kind occur, philosophers and scientists sometimes conclude that because the contending parties cannot settle their differences by straightforward observation, they cannot settle them at all. Sometimes they go further and contend that it does not even make sense in such cases to say that one party rather than another is in the right. In other words they accept (if only implicitly) that the three conditions for relativity have been satisfied. But philosophers or scientists who draw these conclusions are mistaken. The fact that a dispute cannot be settled by straightforward appeal to observation does not mean that it cannot be settled at all. For the natural sciences do not rely on observation alone for distinguishing true from false claims. They look in addition to such things as scope and range of explanation; agreement with other theories and background beliefs; lack of persuasive alternatives; simplicity and economy; ability to handle anomalies; metaphysical gain. There is no case then in the natural sciences for dismissing an assertion or theory as culturally relative on the grounds that disputes concerning it cannot be resolved by simple observation.

The same may now be said of the social sciences when they in turn make reference to things beyond the range of commonsense; when for example they speak of average consumers; of the sub-conscious; of facts which are irreducibly social; of totally free markets; of ideal types, faculties and latent functions. These and other items of their sort, like their counterparts in the natural sciences, give rise on occasion to clashes of opinion which cannot be resolved by recourse to observation alone. But this should not tempt us to treat the opposing claims as having a truth relative only to the individuals, groups or cultures which assert them. For the social sciences are no more dependent exclusively on observation than the natural sciences. They also look to such things as simplicity, agreement with background assumptions and range of explanation.

Because of this, they cannot — or at least they cannot in the absence of new and more convincing arguments — be said to be culturally relative. What is more, there is no reason to believe that they will not progressively settle their disputes. The natural sciences have for the most part settled theirs.

APPENDIX

Throughout this chapter, the claim has been advanced that although the social sciences have a distinguishing *object* (men with their meanings, purposes and so on), they are not radically different from the natural sciences. But since this view is by no means universally accepted, it will be worthwhile to add a brief survey of the principal objections raised against it. (Those readers who *do* accept it may prefer to pass straight on to the next chapter.)

The social sciences and laws

Many critics are hostile to the assimilation of the social sciences to the natural on the grounds that the social sciences are not able to establish *laws*. In this they oppose a long established tradition in the West, running from Comte, through Mill, to such writers as Merton and Homans, and which rather confusingly they label 'positivist'. According to this tradition, the ideal of the social sciences (in emulation of the natural) is to discover and systematise laws governing human behaviour, from which laws it will be possible deductively to 'explain' less general claims.

It should be clear from the conclusions reached in Chapter 2 that to criticise this 'positivist' tradition in the social sciences is not *eo ipso* to criticise the assertion that the social sciences are fundamentally the same as the natural. For it was seen that the establishing of laws is neither the unique pursuit of the natural sciences nor their essentially characterising feature. On the contrary it was argued that the natural sciences are a complex human undertaking, the successes of which are by no means co-extensive with the discovering of laws. To illustrate this point with the use of examples: if the natural sciences had discovered that the heart is a pump, that human beings evolved from other species, that the planets move in orbits round the sun, that there are such things as atoms and viruses, that white light conjoins the colours of the rainbow — if they had discovered such things without establishing *any* exceptionless regularities in nature, they would still be what fundamentally they now are: an inquiry into the nature of physical reality and its basic structures. For this reason it is plainly mistaken to equate the natural sciences with the discovery of laws, and from this premiss to argue that the social sciences must be totally different from the natural.

Further, while as a matter of fact the social sciences have not come up with any laws, the different claim that they are unable to do so of their very nature is not self-evident, and the reasons put forward to support it should be looked at carefully.

The first of these reasons amounts to asserting that there are no human, social universals — that is, no properties shared socially by all men — and that correspondingly there *can* be no universally true statements about men and societies. However, if the arguments of Chapter 1 were sound, this first reason against the possibility of laws in the social sciences is by itself unconvincing, since there *have* to be shared human and social properties — the possession, for example, of common beliefs, abilities and attitudes. If there were not, the social sciences would be unable from the outset to conduct their inter-cultural inquiries. Anthropologists, for example, would be unable to study the beliefs, attitudes and customs of groups if the latter were not already in possession of beliefs and attitudes in common with the anthropologists' in the first place. Indeed it was argued in Chapter 1 that even the nature and content of many of these beliefs must be universal if we are properly to allow their possessors to count as human. The denial of human and social universals therefore is not a good premiss for the denial of social-scientific laws.

The second reason advanced against the possibility of laws in the social sciences is that human beings possess free will. In virtue of this, it is contended, men are capable of ensuring the falsity of any statement which might be proposed as an example of a law. In other words, it is said to be essential to free will that human actions escape the sorts of predictability following upon the existence and knowledge of laws.

If this argument is to be allowed any plausibility at all, it can only be when the notion of free will made use of is that employed by the *non-determinist*. For the (soft) determinist, the philosopher who holds that all occurrences are determined, and that what we call 'free actions' constitute merely a sub-class of those determined occurrences — such a philosopher is committed in advance to the view that if there are laws at all, human actions are as likely as anything to come under them. So the argument can be put forward seriously only by the non-determinist (by the libertarian or the agent-theorist). How much plausibility does it *then* have? Not a great deal. For since the doctrine of non-determined free will is compatible with a belief in the existence of *physical* laws, there are no clear grounds *a priori* for considering the same doctrine to be incompatible with a belief in the existence of *social* laws. To illustrate this point with an example, the claim that a man is non-determinedly free to get up or to stay in bed, is in no way at odds with the claim that what in the end he chooses is done under the constraints of the laws of gravity and conservation of mass-energy. But if in this way a person's free will is able to operate within a framework of physical laws, there seems to be nothing inconsistent in supposing it able to operate within a framework of social laws. From this it follows that the doctrine of free will cannot of itself show that there could not be social-scientific laws.

The third argument comes to the following. Given the nature of the concepts employed in making sense of human affairs, there are no social-scientific statements which we might seriously think of as being true universally — that is, true without exception of all or some class of men. For surely we can always imagine men singly or in groups making sufficient effort to contrive exceptions. Further, given that human actions are essentially the outcome of beliefs and desires ('pro-attitudes'), they seem to escape the range of laws precisely because men's beliefs and desires are so greatly variable. If from period to period and from culture to culture there is endless variety among human beliefs and desires, how can we ever seriously hope to establish laws describing the ways in which men have always acted in the past and will continue to act in the future?

This argument relies on an analysis of the concepts which men use in describing and conducting their affairs. But while we may accept the force of it as it stands, we can still urge that with the introduction of *new* concepts, or with the revision of the old, laws will yet be established. Further, it is far from clear anyway that we can always imagine men contriving exceptions to whatever statements may be put forward as laws. To take an example, it is not implausible to suppose that laws governing the stages of children's cognitive development will be arrived at in the near future. It seems less plausible to suppose that men will be able straight off to contrive exceptions to them. Finally, it is not unreasonable to press for the view that since there are in fact recurring patterns among the actions and interactions of men, there must be fundamental laws underpinning them. If, for example, societies are stratified, it is not unreasonable to assume that this feature is the manifestation of some underlying and universal regularity: that is the sort of assumption made often enough in the natural sciences. Such an underlying regularity might of course turn out to be biological or physical, but there is nothing intrinsically absurd in suggesting that it might turn out to be social.

The further point can be made that significant progress in the natural sciences has usually depended upon the adoption and hammering out of new and technical concepts; and this suggests the possibility that success in formulating social-scientific laws might likewise follow upon the introduction of a suitable set of concepts.

The final and most important argument against the possibility of laws in the social sciences makes appeal to the fact that any universal statement about human affairs, however strongly confirmed in the past, could in principle readily be made false in the future by suitable alterations either to men's physical states or to their environment. Whatever the pattern of men's individual or social behaviour, one or more of such things as disease, radiation, drought, change in the earth's atmosphere, drugs or neuro-surgery could alter them. From this it would seem to follow that there can be no exceptionless regularities, no universal laws governing men's behaviour.

There is a sense in which the point of this argument has to be conceded. It amounts to the incontestable claim that the existence of men in their present form is contingent upon changeable circumstances, and that therefore it cannot be the subject of eternal, unalterable regularities. But this does not entail that humans do not come under discoverable social laws *for as long as they exist in their present nature* and with their present characteristics. In fact, to deny the possibility of laws in such conditions is inconsistent with accepting them in biology and many areas of physics. For the existence of organisms in general is no less contingent than that of men in particular, nor is the existence of much that commonly we count as typical of the physical world. That there is water is contingent. That there exist crystal formations is contingent. At a deeper level, that there are gases is contingent. From all of this it follows that while we accept the actuality of Bragg's and Boyle's laws, we ought not to reject the possibility of social laws.

The social sciences and explanation

The natural and social sciences are often held to differ fundamentally on the grounds that the kinds of understanding and explanation they require are in no sense alike. Winch, for example, has argued that the 'understanding of society is *logically different* from the understanding of nature', and that 'the notion of a human society involves a scheme of concepts which is *logically incompatible* with the kinds of explanation offered in the natural sciences' (italics mine).[12]

It is true that whenever men engage in what we call human actions, more is needed to explain what is going on than a set of statements referring to overt physical occurrences and patterns of behaviour. Reference must be made to such things as what the men in question mean, what they intend, what motivates them, what rules they follow and what rational procedures have led to their present activities. To explain, for example, why the examiner put a tick against the second answer on Smith's mathematics paper, a great deal more is required than appeals to physiology and dynamics. And the same is true in the case of explaining why voters are given pieces of paper at polling-booths, or why Polish people have a traditional fear of Russian expansionist designs. Even the materialist philosopher, if he wishes to refute his opponents, must understand their meanings and the rules that guide their arguments.

But the question now to be asked is this. Does the fact that the social sciences in the above ways require special sorts of explanation exclude their also employing explanations of a kind which are used by the natural sciences?

They are excluded from employing explanations which rely on laws, since (at present) the social sciences have no laws. But is there any reason why they should not work with lesser regularities — with tendencies or probabilities? There would seem to be none. For there is no reason *a priori* against the application of different types of explanation to identical occurrences. On the contrary, we know quite well, to take an example, that the same event can be explained by an appeal to the laws of motion and by an appeal to the rules of a game. 'Why did that piece of ivory move like that?' can be answered by giving its mass and the forces applied to it, and at the same time it can be answered by pointing out that the piece is a knight in a game of chess, moving forward to counter the threat of an opponent's queen. So it *is* possible for a single event to have more than one type of explanation. But can one of these explanations ever consist in an appeal to regularities among human actions? The answer clearly is Yes, since we do as a matter of fact give perfectly acceptable explanations in terms of social-scientific regularities, over and above our explanations in terms of individuals' meanings, rules, intentions and motives. We say, for example, that John's success in passing his examinations is to be explained by his family's social standing, traditional success and obvious enthusiasm for learning. Or we explain the level of income in a group by referring to its educational background and achievements. But even more can be said. Not only do we as a matter of fact appeal to social-scientific regularities of these and other sorts, but often we *have* to if we are to make sense of people's actions. To illustrate this again with an example, let us suppose that John has killed Peter. Let us suppose further that John believed Peter to have seduced his wife and that he was out for revenge. Do we now have sufficient explanation of John's action? Some philosophers hold that we do, and in addition claim that those who think otherwise have not fully understood the meanings of such terms as 'seduce' and 'revenge'.[13] But this seems unsatisfactory. Not every man who believes that his wife has been seduced and is out for revenge goes on to commit murder. So if we do accept the proposed explanation of John's killing Peter, we can do so only if we believe that people in similar circumstances murder with some regularity.

Finally, we often have to appeal to regularities when we wish to decide whether or not to trust a man's explanations of his own actions. Surely there is no way of deciding in these cases except by comparing what a man says with what he *usually does.*

So explanations of human actions do not rule out appeals to regularities: if anything they require them.

The social sciences and the unobservable

The social sciences, if the things said above are correct, are concerned in considerable part with men's meanings, beliefs, desires and intentions. But these, it is sometimes argued, are essentially private and therefore unable to furnish a foundation for the kind of certainty achieved in the natural sciences. In other words, it is said that the social scientist has no direct access to the subject-matter of his inquiries, and that because of this he is prone to errors of a kind and magnitude from which the natural scientist is protected by his open and public procedures.

In spite of the efforts of philosophical behaviourists and others, it has to be conceded that there is a sense in which the subject-matter of the social sciences is private. No social scientist can have direct access, for example, to the thoughts that are going through my mind as I fill in a questionnaire; no social scientist can observe and check on my pains in the way that he can observe and check on my overt behaviour. But all of this could be considered a serious setback only if at the same time the social scientist could be said to have no reliable *indirect* access to his subject-matter. But this surely he does have. Only the extreme philosophical sceptic will think of arguing that we cannot in any way know what goes on in other men's minds, and the social scientist is no more vulnerable than others to this sort of attack. The physicist, for example, needs as much as anyone to know what goes on in the minds of others; to know what his colleagues think and what they mean and intend by their words. So scepticism is a weapon against everyone or against no one: it has no particular relevance to the social scientist.

Of course, the social sciences do have a special problem in that the human thoughts, desires and intentions that they wish to look into are often of a kind that men lie about, conceal or are unable to express. But this sort of difficulty cannot be held to undermine the claim of the social sciences to achieve reliable knowledge. For it is after all only a difficulty, which by patient and persevering investigation, cross-checking and other methods can in great measure be overcome.

It is worth adding that the natural sciences have parallel problems of their own. Many of the central items investigated in such areas as physics, astronomy, geology and biology are as much beyond the direct access of the natural scientist as the thoughts of man are beyond the immediate scrutiny of the social scientist.

The social sciences, precision, experimentation and predictability

The natural sciences are sometimes held to be characterised by their use of experimentation, precise measurement and power of detailed prediction. In this they are also held to contrast with the social sciences.

It is true that the social sciences are limited in the scope and kind of experimentation which they are able to carry out. Sociologists, for example, cannot experiment with their subjects in the way that biologists and physicists can with theirs. Again, the social sciences cannot by the use of precise measurement achieve the success of the natural sciences. For most of the central concepts they work with, and possibly always will work with — kin, class, fear, belief, ceremony and the rest — do not lend themselves to the kind of useful measurement that made sense of motion, atoms and spectra. Lastly, the social sciences are not able to match their supposed rivals in the accuracy and detail of their predictions. Quite the contrary. When sociologists, political scientists and others attempt to make even short-term predictions, they tend notoriously to meet with as little success as the interested layman.

However, these points do not show that there is a major contrast between the natural and the social sciences, nor do they show that the latter are unable to acquire genuine knowledge and provide satisfactory explanations. It was argued in the last chapter that the natural sciences themselves do not in all areas make use of experiment and precise measurement, or come forward with detailed predictions. The theory of evolution by natural selection does not centrally rely on laboratory experiments and close measurement, nor is there much that it can predict concerning the way in which this or that species will develop or decline. Again, there are few experiments that geologists or cosmologists can carry out to repeat the sorts of events which they wish to explain — and as to their grand-scale predictions, these are no more than glorified guesses.

More generally, to recall the open view of the natural sciences put forward in Chapter 2, there are no sharp features contrasting them with the social sciences. Both are engaged in description, generalisation, observation, explanation and (in varying degrees) prediction. Both are theory-laden. And both have background beliefs and suppositions — empirical, logical and metaphysical. This of course is not to say that some areas of the natural sciences do not contrast with some areas of the social. In establishing strict laws, for example, physics contrasts with anthropology and sociology. But then on the same grounds it contrasts with biology, geology and astronomy.

The social sciences and practice

It is often said, especially by Neo-Marxist 'critical theorists', that one of the great tragedies in the development of Western philosophy since the Enlightenment has been the intellectual divorce between theory and practice — between what they prefer to speak of as *theoria* and *praxis* — and between fact and value. They claim that in this respect Anglo-Saxon philosophy has been especially guilty, making it impossible for rational discussion of values to take place and for rational decisions to be made concerning what is to be done. They argue further that a major part of the trouble has been that the natural sciences have unwarrantedly been taken to be the only true kind of knowledge, and they oppose all 'positivistic' attempts to turn the social sciences into a sub-species of them. In the social sciences above all, they insist, theory and practice, fact and value, must be kept inseparable.

It is not clear that these Neo-Marxists have helped in any way to bridge the gaps which they so bitterly oppose. Indeed they are sometimes plainly guilty of opening new ones. Habermas, for example, teaches (disastrously) that 'critique' constitutes a radically different form of knowledge from that pursued in the natural sciences.[14] The next few chapters of this book will bring out, by contrast, that rational and systematic considerations of value are continuous with the task of the natural and the social sciences.

FURTHER READING

*Barbour, I.G. *Issues in Science and Religion,* London, 1966, Chap. 7.

Bernstein, R.J. *The Restructuring of Social and Political Theory,* Oxford, 1976.

Borger, R. and Cioffi, F. *Explanation in the Behavioural Sciences,* Cambridge, 1970.

*Bottomore, T.B. *Sociology,* London, 1962.

Bottomore, T. and Nisbet R. (eds.), *A History of Sociological Analysis,* London, 1979.

Braybrooke, D. *Philosophical Problems of the Social Sciences,* New York, 1965.

Brodbeck, M. *Readings in the Philosophy of the Social Sciences,* New York, 1968.

*Brown, R. *Explanation in Social Science,* London, 1963.

Cohen, M.R. *Reason and Nature,* New York, 1931.

Cunningham, F. *Objectivity in Social Science,* Toronto, 1973.

Dray, W.H. *Philosophy of History,* Englewood Cliffs, N.J., 1964.

Emmett, D. and MacIntyre, A. *Sociological Theory and Philosophical Analysis,* London, 1970.

*Fay, B. *Social Theory and Political Practice,* London, 1975.

Gallie, W.B. *Philosophy and the Historical Understanding,* London, 1964.

Gardiner, P. *Theories of History,* New York, 1959.

*Gibson, Q. *The Logic of Social Enquiry,* London, 1960.

Kaplan, A. *The Conduct of Inquiry — Methodology for Behavioral Sciences,* San Francisco, 1965.

Kaufmann, F. *Methodology in the Social Sciences,* London, 1944.

Keat, R.N. and Urry, J.R. *Social Theory as Science,* London, 1975.

Krimerman, L.I. *The Nature and Scope of Social Science,* New York, 1969.

*Lessnoff, M. *The Structure of Social Science,* London, 1974.

MacIntyre, A. "The Idea of a Social Science", *Proceedings of the Aristotelian Society,* supp.vol., 1967.

Mandelbaum, M. *The Problem of Historical Knowledge,* New York (Torch book ed.), 1967.

Midgley, M. *Beast and Man,* (Methuen), London, 1980.

Mill, J.S. *A System of Logic,* London, 1843, Book 6.

*Nagel, E. *The Structure of Science,* London, 1961, Chaps. 13-15.

Natanson, M. *Philosophy of the Social Sciences,* New York, 1963.

Pap, A. *Introduction to the Philosophy of Science,* Glencoe, Ill., 1962, Chap. 17.

Popper, K. *The Poverty of Historicism,* London, 1957.

*Pratt, V. *The Philosophy of the Social Sciences,* London, 1978.

Rex, J. *Key Problems of Sociological Theory,* London, 1961.

Rickman, H.P. *Understanding and the Human Studies,* London, 1967.

Riley, G. *Values, Objectivity and the Social Sciences,* Reading, Mass., 1974.

Rudner, R.S. *Philosophy of Social Science,* Englewood Cliffs, N.J., 1966.

*Ryan, A. *The Philosophy of the Social Sciences,* London, 1970.

Ryan, A. *The Philosophy of Social Explanation,* London, 1973.

Tennekes, J. *Anthropology, Relativism and Method,* Assen, 1971.

Thorpe, W.H. *Animal Nature and Human Nature,* London, 1974.

Walsh, W.H. *An Introduction to Philosophy of History,* London, 1951.

Wartofsky, M.W. *Conceptual Foundations of Scientific Thought,* New York, 1968.

Weber, M. *The Methodology of the Social Sciences,* Glencoe, Ill., 1949.

Winch, P. *The Idea of a Social Science,* London, 1958.

*Worsley, P. *Introducing Sociology,* Harmondsworth, 2nd ed., 1977.

CHAPTER 4
THE NATURE OF MORALITY

As was stressed in the Introduction, one form of the doctrine of cultural relativism that deserves special examination is ethical or moral cultural relativism: the doctrine that men's beliefs in matters of right and wrong are relative to the groups, cultures or sub-cultures within which those beliefs are acquired. This doctrine deserves special attention for at least three reasons. First, it is among the most widely held and stoutly defended forms of relativism, evidence for it being thought to flow from many sources at once: from history and sociology, for example, or from anthropology and even epistemology. Second, parents, teachers and other interested members of society not infrequently hold that the beliefs acquired by children about what is right and wrong are more important than the beliefs they acquire about such things as the nature of the physical universe or the history of a nation's achievements, and it would be difficult to justify valuing moral beliefs so highly if their truth and consequent authority were held to be no more than local. Third, there is a special difficulty about assessing the claims of ethical relativism, a difficulty which arises from the fact that it is not easy to be sure what the nature of ethics is in the first place. Some philosophers in recent years have held, for example, that when we say such things as, 'Torture is wrong', while grammatically we are uttering statements of fact, in substance we are doing no more than giving expression to our feelings, making plain our attitudes or prescribing and recommending to others this or that mode of conduct. Other philosophers, by contrast, have preserved the view that in such cases we are uttering real statements of fact, but they have not been agreed on what sorts of fact are at issue. Are they facts, for example, about the inner states and feelings of those who utter them? Are they facts about features of the public, physical world? Or are they facts about items belonging to some quite separate realm — a realm of moral values or something of that kind?

Given the diversity and extremity of views on the nature of ethics, it seems that the strength of the relativist's case will depend *inter alia* on which analysis of ethical or moral utterances he wishes to defend. It is consequently impossible seriously to accept or reject ethical relativism without first making plain which analysis is at stake. In other words, a preliminary requirement for a sustained discussion of ethical relativism is an understanding of the nature of ethics or morality itself.

It is the task of the present chapter to help provide that understanding.

The nature of philosophical enquiry

How does one properly go about answering questions like, What is morality? More generally, how does one properly go about answering philosophical questions at all? On this there is no agreed answer. Some philosophers have said that we should consult with dictionaries and common usage. Others that we should turn in upon ourselves, to consult our intuitions or the light within us of natural reason. Others again have urged that the methods of philosophy are proper to that enquiry itself and can be learned only in the company of philosophers, or by assiduously reading their works.

In rejection of these views and in keeping with what has been argued already, it seems more plausible to hold that fundamentally philosophy is the same in kind as any other intellectual venture. The philosopher, like the physicist, the historian or even the mathematician, is confronted with a skein of problems arising from his present beliefs and experiences, and he formulates hypotheses and theories to meet these problems. The only thing that is required of his hypotheses and theories is that they should be the best that are currently available — a point that will be taken up in a moment. It is certainly not required of them that they should prove final and irrevocable, nor that they be able to answer all objections with equal facility. There will always be loose strands.

The point concerning the lack of finality in hypotheses and theories deserves again to be underlined. It amounts to this. While for the most part men hold their beliefs and theories to be true, they do not hold them to be incorrigible, since they do not in the first place imagine themselves to be infallible. The following case will illustrate the point. We hold that today is Tuesday. We do not doubt it. We have no grounds for doubting it. On the other hand, we do not claim infallibility in the matter. We concede that we might be mistaken, since in like circumstances in the past we have in fact been mistaken. There is nothing inconsistent then in holding this and other beliefs to be true (including our theories) while considering them still to be open in principle to correction.

It was said a moment ago that our hypotheses and theories, in whatever area, must always be the best that are currently available to us. But what are to count as the best? The briefest answer to this question is that our best theories are those which, if any, are the most likely to be true. However, this characterisation appears to be formal to the point of emptiness, so we need to add the following sorts of criteria (already familiar from Chapters 2 & 3). Our best theories typically are to be the simplest, yielding the greatest measure of unity in diversity; they should be supported by and make sense of the widest range of our experiences and beliefs; they should be consonant with the largest number of our theories in related areas; they should cause the least unnecessary disturbance to our central ways of conceptualising reality; they should be productive in suggesting yet further theories; they should leave behind them the smallest number of puzzles, anomalies and other unexplained phenomena. It must be underlined, however, that there are no clear-cut hierarchies among these and kindred criteria: we have no means of applying them according to a mechanical calculus. Weightings can be given to them, or to subsets of them, only when due regard has been given to the particular case in hand. There are no prescriptions in advance.

The nature of rationality

The theory concerning the nature of morality to be put forward and argued for in this chapter comes to the following. To behave morally is quite simply to behave rationally in one particular area of human behaviour (yet to be specified). In a word, morality is a species of the genus which we call rationality. Given this proposed definition, the best thing to start with will be the nature of rationality, and consequently the whole of this section will be devoted to it.

For men to be rational is for them to do two sorts of things. First, to hold their beliefs in accordance with the principles and procedures in their possession for reaching the truth, gaining systematic knowledge and attaining and preserving critical understanding. Second, to order their activities in accordance with whatever principles and procedures they have for achieving the optimum number of their aims and objectives.

The rational principles and procedures referred to here are simply those of deductive and inductive logic, and these may be characterised briefly as follows. Deductive logic concerns the kind of relationship which exists between propositions, or sets of propositions, when, if one proposition or set of propositions is true, the other cannot be false. Inductive logic, by contrast, concerns the kind of relationship which exists, when, if one proposition or set of propositions is true, its being true supports the truth of the other but still allows for the possibility of that other's being false. More briefly, two propositions are deductively related if the truth of one conclusively ensures the truth of the other; two propositions, by contrast, are inductively related, if the truth of one supports, but does not conclusively ensure the truth of the other. (The notion of induction here is clearly much wider than that of enumerative induction discussed in Chapter 2.)

The examples usually given of propositions which stand in deductive relationships and so form deductive arguments, are those which contain such small words as 'and', 'if', 'or', 'not'; words often referred to as 'logical particles'. It has on occasion been suggested by philosophers that deduction hinges entirely on these logical particles: that when asked why deductive relationships hold at all, we should reply that they hold in virtue of the meanings of 'if', 'not', 'and', 'or'. This suggestion has in turn led at times to the belief that at bottom there is something trivial about deduction: that while its counterpart, induction, comes to grips with the world, helps us to understand it and enables us to make predictions concerning it, deduction merely displays the manner in which words, terms or meanings are interrelated.

The question of this supposed triviality of deduction will be pursued later. What in the meantime needs to be made clear is that at the most *some* deductive relationships could be explained by reference to logical particles. Others undoubtedly hinge on what may be termed content-words. For example, the proposition, 'This box is coloured', deductively follows from the proposition, 'This box is red'. But if we wish to explain this deduction, we cannot appeal to logical particles, since on this occasion none have been made use of. The relevant words or terms to be singled out are 'coloured' and 'red'.

Before we go further, it will be useful if we pause for a moment and attempt to answer the following question. When it is said that deduction hinges on the meanings of logical particles and (or) content-words, is anything really being said of consequence, given that induction also in some sense hinges on the meanings of the words or terms it employs? In answer to this it is sometimes replied that deductive, unlike inductive, relationships exist *solely* in virtue of the meanings of the terms they employ. But this is scarcely more than a verbal shuffle, explaining little. For if we assert that deductive relationships form part of the meanings of terms, all that we are doing is, so to speak, *locate* them. On the other hand, if we hold that deductive relationships do not form part of the meanings of terms, but simply that they always and necessarily accompany them, this time we are doing no more than saying what they *go with*; again we are not explaining them. So it seems *irreducibly* true that where there are meanings there are deductive relationships, and the other way round; just as where there are particulars there are universals and the other way round. Each requires, neither is able to explain, the other.

To return to answering our original question. In the light of what has just been said, if we claim that deductive relationships in some special fashion hinge on the meanings of terms, we can only have in mind something like the following. A person who understands the meanings of the terms employed in propositions which are deductively related is *eo ipso* able to perceive the deductive relationship involved, by reflecting on the meanings of the terms and without recourse to further experience of the world. To make use of the examples that were introduced a moment ago, someone who understands the meanings of the terms 'red' and 'coloured' also understands that when these terms appear, and as they appear, in the propositions cited, those propositions are related deductively. Conversely, if someone believes that a box may be red without being coloured, we say that he does not understand either one or both of the terms 'red' and 'coloured' (assuming of course that he understands the rest). But none of this, to repeat, *explains* the relation of deduction; at the most it fastens on to certain necessary conditions for its recognition.

So far I have said something about the nature of rationality, extensionally defining it in terms of inductive and deductive logic. Then, having characterised these two branches of logic, I have focused principally on the nature and meaning of the deductive relationship. The reason for this is that the underpinning of morality as rationality will be seen to consist in a set of deductive relationships or arguments (together with some definitions). This will be made plain in the following section; meanwhile, there is further preliminary work to be done, this time concerning the notion of 'having reasons for doing things'.

It will be useful in dealing with this point to begin with some semi-abstract examples.

Example 1.
(i)   John has x as a goal.
(ii)   Conclusion: John has a reason for pursuing x.

Example 2.
(i)   John has x as a goal.
(ii)   The reason that John has for pursuing x is better than any reason John has for pursuing something else instead; or for doing nothing at all.[1]
(iii)   Conclusion: John ought to pursue x; John would be irrational not to pursue x.

Example 3.
(i)   x is one of John's aversions.
(ii)   The reason that John has for avoiding x is better than any reason that John has for doing something else instead.
(iii)   Conclusion: John ought to avoid x; John would be irrational not to avoid x.

These examples have been chosen to illustrate the foundations of morality as rationality, and because of this they call for a number of comments.

First, while they are semi-abstract in nature, they can very easily be given flesh. The first example, for instance, can be instantiated in the following way:

(i)   John has a desire to drink.
(ii)   Conclusion: John has a reason for taking the steps necessary to get a drink.

Similar instantiations can readily be found for the other examples.

Second, they are examples of the sort of deductive relationship or argument which hinges not on logical particles but on content-words (goal, aversion, reason, avoid, ought).

Third, like other examples of deductive relationships they depend on the

66

meanings of terms, at least in the epistemic sense outlined earlier on: namely, we would say of someone who denied that these deductive relationships hold that he did not understand the terms employed.

This particular point will bear elaboration. To understand what it is for a person to have a goal, and at the same time to understand what it is for a person to have a reason for pursuing or attaining something, is also and at once to understand that if a person has a goal, x, he has *eo ipso* a reason for pursuing x. And parallel things may be said concerning aversions and having reasons for avoiding them. However, there is more to understanding the expression 'having a reason' than perceiving its simple connections with terms such as 'goal' and 'aversion'. This is because reasons for doing or avoiding things are usually, if not always, only *prima facie* reasons. By this I mean that if we have a reason for doing (or avoiding) x, it does not follow that we ought to do (or avoid) x, since there may well be compelling reasons for doing y instead, or for simply doing nothing. That is why often we need to deliberate. To illustrate the point: I may have several good reasons for going to Sydney next week. I may very much like Sydney; I may have friends that I wish to visit there; I may have business to transact there. On the other hand, I may have several good reasons for staying in Hobart. I may be busy here; I may have promised to do a number of things here which ought not to be postponed; I may hate travelling anyway. Given this conflict of reasons, I deliberate. That is, I ask myself *not* 'What do I have reasons for doing?' — obviously I have reasons for doing both — but, 'What in the circumstances ought I to do?' And I discover what I ought to do — I discover that I ought to do this thing, x, rather than some other thing, y — as soon as I come to have serious grounds for believing that the reasons I have for doing x are better than the reasons I have for doing y, or for doing nothing at all. That is what 'ought' means.

The fourth comment to be made is brief and obvious, but fundamental. It is that the notion of 'having reasons for doing (or avoiding) things' forms part, indeed nearly the whole, of the wider notion of what it is to be a man at all. For men are essentially the sorts of beings that have conscious goals: that is, they have desires, wants, loves, needs, hopes and aspirations. Equally they have aversions; they have fears, anxieties, hates, revulsions and hostilities. In summary, men are creatures that have conscious *aims*; some of these being positive, some negative. But it is precisely the having of such aims which enables men to be rational in their activities as well as in their beliefs. Put more formally: a man has a reason for pursuing or avoiding x if and only if x is one of his aims,[2] or x is a suitable means for attaining one of his aims. Put more tersely: where there are no aims, there are no rational activities; where there are no rational activities, there are no men.

The fifth comment to be made constitutes an attempt to meet the objection that was foreshadowed earlier: namely, that deductive relations are in some sort trivial. This objection may now be re-worded (rather more liberally) as follows. All that has been done so far is to trace out certain deductive relations and to put forward sets of definitions (of rationality, humanity, deduction and so forth). All that has been looked at, then, is the meaning of words. But this sort of procedure provides very shaky foundations for morality, since the meanings of words are notoriously just matters of convention.

The claim here that meanings of words are just matters of convention is frequently taken to carry with it the suggestion that meanings are therefore subject to alteration whenever and in whatever manner we desire. Moreover, this suggestion seems to be supported in countless examples. The precise number of colour words we employ, for instance, and the correspondingly quasi-permanent distinctions that these bring with them, are clearly subject to alteration at whim. If we wish to introduce a new colour-chart or to extend the charts already in existence, there is nothing to prevent us apart from our own choices. And the same is true for the ranges of words which we employ in distinguishing sounds, smells, tastes and shapes. Again we are at liberty to create as many new words as we wish, and to stipulate their meanings as we want. The meanings of words, in short, are up to us.

This objection however will not do. For the meanings of words are *not* up to us; at least in the important sense that we can neither do without many of our words — more properly, without the concepts which those words express — nor can we significantly alter them without at the same time so altering a host of others that our understanding collapses altogether.

This point may be illustrated from some arguments that were deployed in Chapter 1. There it was brought out that we can have no understanding of reality without having beliefs concerning it, and that in turn we cannot possess beliefs without at the same time possessing the following closely-knit set of concepts: *falsity, negation, assertion, contradiction, exclusion, alternation, entailment*. Again, given the nature of the world we inhabit, we can acquire no systematic understanding of it without possessing an additional set of concepts to cover the process both of acquiring reasons for beliefs and of assessing those reasons — for the purpose of gauging what we ought, and what we ought not, to believe. We ought to believe a proposition, p, to be true if and only if the reasons we have for believing p to be true are better than any reasons we have for believing the truth of some incompatible proposition, q, instead; or simply for believing the truth of not-p. This definition nicely summarises the fact that so many of our concepts (and the words that express them) — concepts like *proposition, belief, truth, negation* and *reason* — are not *simply* matters of what we mean by our words, if by this is intended that we can either dispense with them or significantly alter them at will. Should anyone claim the contrary, the onus is with him to provide a rival set of concepts.

What has been said concerning belief and the having of reasons for belief can now be extended to acting and to the having of reasons for acting. Just as we cannot rationally hold beliefs unless first we possess a set of concepts which in the main are irreplaceable and unalterable, so we cannot rationally engage in activities without possessing a parallel set of concepts, concepts to include among others: *doing, avoiding, having aims, having reasons for acting, having better reasons for doing this rather than that.* These concepts and the words expressing them, like those surrounding *belief*, cannot be dismissed as matters of pure convention, nor as matters merely of the meanings of words, if by this is meant that we have the same sort of control over them as we have, for example, over the number of colour words that we choose to work with. These concepts are so fundamental, so deeply rooted in the ways in which we conceive of ourselves and of the world around us, that to be without them is to be without understanding.

The outcome of all this is that to argue that the ultimate foundation of morality consists in a set of definitions and deductive relations, is not to argue that our moral beliefs are merely matters of convention, matters that rest upon whim and fancy.

The sixth comment to be made has the purpose of drawing attention to a distinction of terminology which is often overlooked: the distinction between its being rational to do this or that, and its being irrational not to.

It was argued earlier on that to say of someone, John, that John ought to do x, is to say that it would be against reason or irrational of John *not* to do x. But to say the latter is quite different from saying that it would not be against reason for John to do x, or that it would be rational for him to do x. It is rational for us to do x when we have a good reason for doing x, and no clearly compelling reason for not doing x. By contrast, it is irrational for us *not* to do x when, not merely do we have a good reason for doing x, and no clear reason for not doing x, but the reason we have for doing x is better than any reason we have for doing y instead. An example will make the distinction plain. It would be perfectly rational for me to buy a bottle of champagne this evening, since I have at least one good reason for doing so, namely that I like champagne; and I have no compelling reason for not doing so. But it would not be irrational of me not to make this purchase, since my reasons for doing so are not clearly better than the reasons I have for spending my money on something else, or for simply saving it. In other words, there is some sort of genuine balance of reasons here, and I have in consequence a real choice. The application of this to morality will be that our having good moral reasons for doing this or that does not entail that we ought to do it.

The final comment is this. In each case, the examples quoted refer to *individuals* as having reasons for doing or avoiding things. But if individuals may properly be said to have reasons and rational obligations, so may groups of individuals. To allow this is not to commit us to an ontology embracing the existence of group-minds over and above the minds of individuals. It is to allow no more than is quite properly allowed when we assert such things as, 'The Australian team ought to have batted first against India in the final test', or, 'England had good reasons for going to war against Nazi Germany in 1939'.

However, what needs to be understood is this. While what any given group has reasons for doing must be based on the aims of its individual members, its aims are not necessarily the mere sum of its members' aims. Or, to express this by employing the formal mode: the statement, 'Group G has reasons R for doing x', cannot be reduced to an exhaustive conjunction of statements, each referring to a different member of the group and having the form: 'Individual member M has reasons R for doing x'.

Put more plainly, we can only argue as follows.

(i)   The members (all, most, a significant number) of Group G have in common a set of aims, A, of the kind that cannot be attained without co-operation.

(ii)   G has a reason for engaging in co-operative activity for the purpose of attaining A (from premiss (i)).

(iii)   The reason that G has for engaging in co-operative activity for the purpose of attaining A is better than any reasons G has for doing something else instead, or for doing nothing at all.

(iv)   Conclusion: G ought to engage in co-operative activity for the purpose of attaining A; G would be irrational not so to co-operate.

What we cannot do is derive from these premisses a conclusion stating that each and every member of G ought to engage in co-operative activity. For frequently there occur clashes between the interests of a group and the interests of this or that member of the group, and consequently between what the one and the other ought to do.

This fact is of major importance in moral questions, and will be returned to in detail. Even at the present stage however, an expansion of one of the above examples will be useful by way of illustrating the sort of clash that is at issue. England may have had excellent reasons in 1939 not only for declaring war on Nazi Germany but for introducing conscription and for passing other laws temporarily restricting the liberties of its citizens. Any given individual, John Smith, in turn may have had excellent reasons for approving of those laws. He may, for example, earnestly have desired Germany's defeat. But it does not follow that John Smith could not at the same time have had excellent reasons for not himself complying with the laws passed. Provided that the majority of citizens obeyed the laws and thus fulfilled the conditions necessary for bringing about Germany's defeat, it may well have been in Smith's individual interests, and therefore rational for him, to avoid compliance with the law. Individual-rationality, then, does not always coincide with group-rationality.

The nature of morality

The nature of morality itself can now be turned to, and stated in the following

70

terms. *To act morally is to act in accordance with a set of rational principles, on the basis of which a group of men typically orders or manages the behaviour of its members — whenever that behaviour is of a kind to affect others — with a view to solving the problems which arise on the one hand from men's having aversions, that is, sufferings, pains and other frustrations; and on the other hand from their having ends or goals which stem from their needs, wants, desires and interests.*

Before this theory of the nature of morality is argued for in detail, it will be useful to bear in mind the following preliminary points.

First, no special sort of rationality is at issue here. What distinguishes moral claims and principles from those of physics, history, mathematics or whatever, is not a separate rationality or logic, but what men's universal rationality is *applied* to. In other words, the object, not the logic, distinguishes morality.

The second point is this. It was argued briefly in the last section that what is rational for a given group is not always rational for each and every member of that group. In the light of this, and for reasons that later should become plain, on the present theory morality is characterised as a set of principles which are rational *primarily* within and for a given group: only *derivatively* for individual members of that group. That is, morality is the rationality of a group, not of individuals *qua* individuals. Thus, when we say of an individual that he is acting morally, we mean that he is acting in accordance with what is rational for the group or society to which he belongs. Because of this, central moral utterances, while really they are statements of fact, are often treated and interpreted as prescriptions, rules or commands. For, not unnaturally, behaviour which a society rationally judges to be in its interests, is behaviour which that society will also seek to enjoin and impose upon its members.

Third, all moral statements are, or may be translated into, statements revolving around the basic terms: *reason, irrational.* 'Men ought to keep their promises', for example, may be translated into: 'It is irrational for men not to keep their promises'. 'It is good that men should help their neighbours', may be translated into: 'There are sound reasons why men should help their neighbours'. 'Men have a right to be treated as equals', may be translated into: 'It would be irrational for a society not to uphold the claims of its members to being treated as equals'. 'Thou shall not kill', is a command parasitic on the statement, 'It is irrational for men to kill'. And so on.

To turn now to the principal argument that supports the present theory of morality as rationality. It may be developed as follows.

I. Men have numerous aversions or objects of aversion: that is, there are many things which they dislike, recoil from and seek to avoid. At the same time and parallel to these there are numerous things which men like, incline towards and pursue. Their aversions include such things as pains, fears, humiliations and disappointments, and they arise from three quite distinct sources: from the non-human environment (earthquakes, floods and so forth); from clashes among men themselves which result in competition and warfare; from strifes and contentions within the souls of individual men. Their goals include such things as loves, hopes, longings, aspirations and ambitions, and they arise from similar sources.

II. In addition to their having these sorts of aims (goals and aversions) men are rational; and part of what is meant by saying that they are rational, as was argued in recent paragraphs, is that when there is a group of individuals severally having aims which can be achieved only by co-operation, and these aims are what from now on may conveniently be termed 'overriding', that is, when the reasons for pursuing them are clearly better than any reasons for pursuing some other aims instead (or for pursuing nothing at all), it would be irrational for that group not to engage in co-operative activity for the purpose of attaining the aims at stake. Given the circumstances then in which men find themselves, and given their nature, it would typically be irrational for any human group not to co-operate towards forestalling its individual members' overriding aversions, and towards furthering the realisation of their overriding goals.

The sort of co-operation that is rationally binding here has several components. It requires that a group, both corporately in its representatives (if it has any) and in the generality of its members, refrain from acting in ways to increase the sum of its individuals' overriding aversions. It requires in parallel fashion that the same group act positively to bring about the optimum realisation of its individuals' goals. Finally, it requires that the group corporately take whatever steps are necessary to ensure, by encouragement or by force, that in the absence of special considerations each and every member play his part in the co-operation. This last requirement is justified on the grounds that if it would be irrational not to pursue certain aims, it would *eo ipso* be irrational not to pursue the means necessary for the attainment of those aims.

The argument so far may be summarised in the following three sentences. Men have aims. Men are rational. Men ought therefore to co-operate in furthering their aims. What is yet to be shown is that the sort of co-operation at issue can plausibly be identified with morality, and further, if and given that it can, that the resulting theory is better than its rivals. Before we pursue these final points, however, we need to take a more detailed look at the problem already touched on twice before — the problem of the conflict that sometimes arises between what is rational for a given group and what is rational for this or that individual within the group.

If in any given group each and every individual actually desires to co-operate and positively enjoys playing his part, or at least feels shame at standing aloof, it follows not only that it would be irrational for the group not to engage in co-operation, but that it would be irrational for each and every individual not to contribute to that co-operation; provided as usual that the desires in point are not outweighed by others. However, the case is quite

72

different when this or that individual, while wanting co-operation to exist within his group or society on the grounds that he benefits from it, on the one hand has no desire himself to contribute to it, and on the other hand has very good grounds for believing that no ill effects will befall him if he does not contribute.

An example may be useful. Most present-day complex societies make use of a system of rates and taxes, and require of their members in general that they co-operate by making a contribution. Each individual benefits, or at least is in a position to benefit, from the existence of this kind of co-operation – benefits from education, street-lighting, water-supplies, and so on – and because of this, each individual has reasons for approving of the co-operation. The sedulous tax-avoider is no exception; indeed he has more reason than most for approving of the co-operation, since he benefits from it without personal cost. He can therefore quite validly reflect both that it would be irrational for the society of which he is a member not to maintain a system of taxes, and that it would be irrational for him not to approve of it. Nonetheless he may have no inclination himself to contribute, and he may have good reasons for believing that no harm will come to him, and no danger to the system, from his not contributing. In such a case not only does he have good reasons for not contributing, but in the absence of counter-vailing and overriding reasons he would be irrational if he did contribute.

An objection to this conclusion is sometimes raised along the following lines. It is clear that it would be irrational for the kinds of society described not to have a system of taxes, and it is equally clear that no such system can exist unless individuals contribute to it. But no individual *qua* individual is different from any other, and therefore, given that each individual benefits, or stands to benefit, each individual ought to contribute, would be irrational not to contribute.

This objection can be met in two ways. It can be pointed out that an individual can see himself under more than one description. He can see himself under the description of 'one member of society, no different *qua* member from any other', and if he sees himself in this light he will correctly judge that he ought to contribute. But equally well he can see himself under the description of: 'John Smith, *this individual* whose co-operation is not needed for the realisation of the aims of his society, and who will continue to benefit without contribution'. If he sees himself in the latter light, and if again there are no adequately countervailing reasons, he will correctly judge that he ought not to contribute, that he would be irrational to do so. The second way of meeting the objection is similar, but looks first at the way in which groups achieve their ends. It is this. The sole justification of a group's co-operation is the fulfilling of certain aims. But these aims can be, and usually are, fulfilled without the co-operation of each and every individual. Given the right circumstances then, it is not irrational for a particular individual to regard himself as an exception, and consequently to withhold co-operation.

73

This conflict arising on occasion between group-rationality and individual-rationality accounts for some of the difficulties and most of the confusions that surround attempts to answer the question, 'Why should I be moral?', and given the obvious importance of this question, it will be best not to put off considering it.

When several persons ask, each of himself, 'Why should I be moral?', they do not necessarily have in mind the same sort of problem. One may have in mind a question rather like, 'Why should I vote for the Democratic Party?', where he wants to know such things as what that party's platform is, what its past record is and what its outlook. In a word, he wants to know what the Democratic Party is all about. Similarly, a person may ask why he should be moral not because the seeds of rebellion are germinating within him, but because he feels that he is not sufficiently clear about morality, and hopes to learn more about what sort of thing it really is. Another person may ask the question because he is indeed in rebellion, but only against this or that specific moral belief, from which he then unthinkingly generalises. Yet a further person may ask the question because he demands to know if there is — or because he doubts if there is — a sufficient motivation for *his* behaving morally. This person in the present context is the most interesting. What are we to say to him?

If like most people he has altruistic feelings and inclinations which extend to the generality of people in his society, it may be pointed out to him that to behave morally is precisely to satisfy these inclinations; since to behave morally is to play a part in the furthering of men's goals and the lessening of their frustrations. If on the other hand he is, or claims to be, entirely without altruistic feelings, it may be pointed out to him that if everyone behaved without regard to morality, he, like the rest, would lose the benefits of living in an orderly society; or he may be reminded of the countless ways that society has, from mild to violent, of dealing with those who do not behave morally. But neither of these points may move him. For concerning the second he may be prepared to take a risk; and concerning the first he may justly reply that it begs the question. For it is true that if everybody ceased to behave with regard to morality society would no longer be the sort of co-operative affair that benefits everyone. But it is not true that society would cease to be that sort of affair if this or that questioner, John Smith, *in isolation* stopped behaving morally. And the question, after all, was why John Smith, not the generality of men, should be moral.

In the end we have to face the fact that if John Smith has neither altruistic nor selfish interests moving him to co-operate with others, there is nothing satisfactory that we can say to him in answer to his question: Why should I be moral? But to face this fact is important. It serves to remind us that every society should ensure at least the following. First, that its members be brought up to see themselves as members and not as isolated individuals. Second, that its members be educated to have feelings and sympathies for

74

others. Third, that adequate measures be taken where necessary to compel those whose interests would otherwise favour their behaving immorally. In other words, it serves to remind us — to make use of a slogan — that first and foremost 'morality belongs to society'.

We can now return to the mainstream of the argument. The conclusion reached so far is that any society would be irrational not to co-operate for the furthering of its members' aims. What next is to be argued for is that it is plausible to identify this form of rational co-operation with morality.

This cannot be done exhaustively within the compass of a page or two, but what can effectively be done is this. It can be shown that what most people will agree to as obvious paradigms of true moral beliefs are also beliefs concerning ways in which it is rational for a society or group of men to behave, or irrational not to behave. Most people will agree, for example, that the following are clear cases, if any are, of what morally men ought not to do. Men ought not to kill others. Men ought not to maim others. Men ought not to torture others. Men ought not to starve others. Men ought not to lie to others. But that these instances of what men ought not to do form a central part of the rational co-operation that is under discussion can briefly be shown in the following way.

Typically, men as individuals have a strong aversion to being killed, maimed, tortured, starved and lied to. But if, in whatever society they belong to, they co-operate in the ways outlined earlier on to prevent the occurrence of these ills, each individual member of the society will thereby benefit, or at least will stand so to benefit. From this it follows that men have good reasons to co-operate on these sorts of issues. But there is more. Given the strength of their aversion to being killed, tortured and so on, men, again typically, are not likely ever to possess better reasons for *not* co-operating in these matters. From this in turn it follows that men ought to co-operate, that it would be irrational for them not to.[3] Rational behaviour on these points then turns out to be co-extensive with moral behaviour, and the theory that morality is rationality is seen to fit at least the more obvious paradigms.

The task of showing that other, indeed most, widely accepted moral beliefs accord well with the present theory of morality can with justification be left for the present, to be taken up later; for the purpose of the present chapter is merely to bring out the nature of morality, not to examine all of its applications. A number of related points may also conveniently be left till later: for example, that moral obligations when stated generally are but *prima facie* obligations; that no moral principles are without possible exceptions; that the circumstances to which moral principles have application vary considerably from society to society.

What needs to be done at present is to complete the principal argument in hand by bringing out however briefly what are the advantages to this theory of morality as rationality.

The following are the chief advantages of the theory of morality as rationality.

The theory rejects the claim that moral statements are merely descriptions of the feelings or other subjective states of those who utter them. It rejects equally the claim that moral statements are not genuinely statements, but disguised commands, prescriptions or expressions of emotion. These claims do not accord well with the views of commonsense or common language, and therefore any theory which, like the present, rejects them is a theory which at least to that extent supports commonsense. And this surely is a point in its favour. For philosophy, like every other systematic attempt at theorising, has to start from the world of commonsense, and should depart from it only when compelled. The present theory shows that in what concerns the objectivity of morals it is not so compelled.

Not only does the present theory support the commonsense view that moral statements are statements of objective fact, but it shows how they can be interpreted as statements of plain and unmysterious fact. They do not, for example, need to be taken as facts requiring the intuition of a special faculty; nor do they need to be seen as so much beyond analysis that they allow for no rational discussion when conflicts arise.

Again, the theory has the attraction of being simple. In this it resembles the doctrine of utilitarianism, but manages to avoid the excessive narrowness of the latter. For while utilitarianism relies on a supposed *single* state or disposition of mind to be aimed at, namely happiness, the 'purpose' of morality on the present theory is the balancing out of all sorts of human aims and interests.

The theory offers a genuine chance of agreement among men over what is right and wrong, at least on fundamental issues. For if men as men have certain basic interests in common and, again as men, are rational, they must have a more than even chance of reaching agreement on moral principles. No doubt there are many obstacles to this reaching of agreement — ignorance, prejudice, undeveloped reasoning skills and so on — but no such obstacles need be permanent. Given that morality is an application of rationality, progress in it is as much to be expected and hoped for as it is where rationality is concerned with the systematising of our beliefs about the physical world.

This question of the possibility of agreement in matters of morals, a question which will be taken up in detail in the next chapter, is important in its own right. It is also important in countering the accusation that the moral objectivist is of necessity authoritarian. The present theory has shown that this is not so; it has shown that the court of appeal in morality is not persons at all but reason.

To conclude on these points. The theory of morality as rationality satisfies the following criteria for being considered the best at present available to us.

In more respects than most it accords with commonsense; it introduces few if any changes to our basic ways of conceptualising; it is simple in that it appeals to only one central principle; it increases the amount of unity in our understanding, arguing for morality as a species under the genus *rationality*; it forms part of a network of theories which attempt to make sense of reality without having recourse to mysterious epistemologies or ontologies; it leaves behind it the fewest puzzles and perplexities.

On the other hand, like all theories, it gives rise to objections, and it will be helpful before concluding this chapter to look at the one of these that is the most serious.

A prima facie obvious objection to the view of morality as a species of rationality

The most serious objection is this. The present theory of morality as rationality licenses *inter alia* the persecution of minorities. For in essence the theory is that given the way men are, with their diverse aims and their ability to reason, it would be irrational of them not to co-operate by so ordering their behaviour that it furthers their aims. But it does not follow from this that it would be irrational of them not to co-operate in furthering the aims of *each and every member*, or *each and every subset of members*. Put more bluntly, the theory allows a society to ignore the interests of its minorities if it suits its purpose to do so; and this includes at the extreme enslaving or killing them.

It may initially be replied to this that in most cases, some would say in all cases, it *is* irrational for a society totally to ignore the interests of its minorities. First, because most societies are made up of people who have at least some sympathy for their fellow men, and therefore do not *wish* to see them persecuted. Second, because minorities are often able to hit back and take revenge. Third, because tolerance often pays handsomely anyway. Fourth, because other societies are likely to intervene. Fifth, because men who persecute today may well constitute a minority tomorrow. And so on. However, while because of these points there may be few cases where a society would not be irrational to ignore the interests of the subsets of its members (or, *mutatis mutandis*, the interests of people in other societies), surely there *are some*. Surely, that is, there are cases where a society will very plausibly judge that it is not against its interests to override its minorities; where it has no serious grounds for fearing retribution. The Romans' treatment of the druids on Mona might serve as an example of such a case, or the Normans' treatment of the Saxons (the latter however forming a minority in point of power rather than number). In brief, then, the present theory of morality leaves room for kinds of behaviour that are not infrequently held to be paradigms of what is *immoral*.

I think that this has to be admitted, but I also think that the following points should be borne in mind.

Not many men in fact are devoid of altruistic feelings. Indeed it is plausible to argue that if many were, the human species would not have survived. But if men generally have altruistic feelings and interests, then even on the theory of morality as rationality they ought not to override the interests of their minorities except in cases of unusual provocation. In other words, the present theory of morality forbids and sanctions much the same as others.

In Western civilisation consideration for the interests of *all* men did not come to be seen as a question of morality until the time of the Stoics. More important, the Stoics based their views on the metaphysical and religious belief that all men, even slaves, possessed within them a spark of the divinity. This seems to suggest that without the backing of special beliefs it is not an obligation of rationality (not a matter of morality therefore) that each and every man's interests should be treated with respect.

While the theory of morality as rationality does not *of itself* enjoin consideration for the interests of each and every individual, it is of course in no way incompatible with such consideration *as an ideal*. For ideals, if nothing else, are what men strongly desire to pursue.

It is not an unmitigated evil to acknowledge that groups of men may at times quite rationally ignore the interests of minorities. On the contrary it should serve to remind us of one of the more obvious lessons of history: that frequently men must fight if they wish to obtain rights. That is (on the present theory of morality), men must fight if they wish to make it irrational for the majority to ignore them.

There are in any case *no* theories of morality which as such entail that men should consider with respect the interests of each and every individual.[4] It is notorious that utilitarianism, if taken seriously, does not. Intuitionism, less notoriously but not less certainly, does not: as a theory it leaves quite open what is to be intuited. Emotivism and prescriptivism do not; for similar reasons. Finally, theories making morality matters of divine command do not. One can easily imagine what sorts of precept might issue from the thrones of Mars or Thor.

A final point here is this. It may be objected that, in spite of all that has now been said by way of mitigation, there is still something utterly unacceptable about a theory allowing the fundamental claims of minorities, if only on occasion, to be overridden. But let us ask what 'utterly unacceptable' means in this context. Surely it means (among other things) that men feel a deep-seated objection and natural aversion to the oppression of minority interests. But if this is true (and, allowing for exceptions, it probably is), it does not follow that we need a theory of morality any different from the one put forward in this chapter. For, according to that theory, if the oppression of minorities is a general object of aversion, it is *eo ipso* immoral: men would be irrational not to co-operate in attempting to lessen its occurrence. In other words, however widely the overriding of minority interests is held to be counter-intuitive, this does nothing to threaten the theory of morality as a form of rationality. On the contrary, the latter can both absorb and give an account of it.

The adaptability of the present theory

In addition to the particular objection concerning the oppression of minorities that has just been explained, there is a more general argument likely to be advanced against a theory of morality as rationality: namely, that it makes morality an affair of the inner feelings and states of men (of their strivings, desires and aversions), rather than of objective and independent values.

However, to this objection it may be replied that while in the present chapter undoubtedly considerable stress has been placed on the inner nature of man and therefore on his basic common goals and aversions, there is nothing in this which makes a theory of morality as rationality incompatible with an objectivist and even Platonically transcendent view of it. To illustrate the point, let us assume for the moment that Plato was right in positing the existence of the Form of the Good; and let us assume further that there are communities of men who are aware of that Good, and feel the attractive power that Plato attributed to it. Surely such communities would be irrational not to co-operate in furthering the pursuit of that Good, and the pursuit of whatever human activities might reflect it. It would be just as irrational of them not to pursue such an overriding and transcendent good, as it would for them, when aware of some intense pain and its repellent nature not to co-operate in avoiding it. So the existence of objective and even transcendent values, if there are such things, does not of itself tell against a theory of morality as rationality. Rationality, in a word, is not synonymous with expediency.

FURTHER READING

*Ayer, A.J. *Language, Truth and Logic*, London, 1936, Chap. 6.
Baier, K. *The Moral Point of View*, New York, 1958.
*Benn, S.I. & Peters, R.S. *Social Principles and the Democratic State*, London, 1959, Chaps 2, 4, 5, 11, 12.
*Ewing, A.C. *Ethics*, London, 1953.
Ewing, A.C. *Second Thoughts in Moral Philosophy*, London, 1959.
Foot, P. *Theories of Ethics* (Oxford Readings), Oxford, 1967.
*Frankena, W.K. *Ethics*, Englewood Cliffs, N.J., 1963.
Gert, B. *The Moral Rules*, New York, 1966.
MacIntyre, A. *A Short History of Ethics*, London, 1967.
*Mackie, J.L. *Ethics*, Harmondsworth, 1977..
*Popkin, R.H. & Stroll, A. *Philosophy Made Simple*, London, 1969.
Smart, J.J.C. & Williams, B. *Utilitarianism For and Against*, Cambridge, 1973.
*Warnock, G.J. *Contemporary Moral Philosophy*, London, 1967.
Warnock, G.J. *The Object of Morality*, London, 1971.
Warnock, M. *Ethics Since 1900*, Oxford, 1960.

CHAPTER 5
ETHICAL CULTURAL RELATIVISM

Given that we now have a reasonable understanding of what is meant by ethics or morality, we can turn to asking whether there are any serious grounds for believing in ethical or moral cultural relativism.

As was mentioned briefly in the last chapter, in one form or other the doctrine of ethical relativism is fairly widespread, and it is often welcomed on the supposition that it justifies and furthers the practice of tolerance. For, it is argued, if no culture's moral beliefs may be said to be true in contrast with any other's, there can be no grounds for being critical of the moral beliefs of others: men ought therefore to be tolerant. If Eskimos approve of the killing of infants, invalids and the aged, it follows on the supposition of the truth of cultural relativism that we can have no grounds for saying that the Eskimos are wrong and that others by contrast are right. We have *a fortiori* no rational grounds for being intolerant of the Eskimos.

However, if this is one way of seeing ethical relativism, there is another. Instead of being viewed as the enlightened and progressive champion of tolerance, it may be seen as a formidable barrier to rational agreement. For it holds that there are, and can be, no common intercultural grounds on which to settle men's differences. Consequently it encourages hostile parties to believe that their several moral views are as correct and as praiseworthy as those of their opponents.

In this chapter it will be argued that in which ever way it is viewed, the doctrine of ethical cultural relativism is untenable. However, before we come to the arguments in favour of this claim, it will be useful to recall and extend some of the points that were made in Chapter 1.

First, the general characterisation of ethical cultural relativism is as follows. To say that an ethical or moral statement is culturally relative is to say that it is not complete until it makes an appropriate reference to at least one culture. For example, the statement, as it stands, that killing is wrong is incomplete. It requires to be filled out with a reference to a culture or cultures, just as much as the statement that John is taller requires to be filled out with a reference to this or that person or persons, or something of the sort.

Second, when ethical relativism is discussed, what often turns out to be at issue is that restricted and perhaps moderate claim that some moral statements are relative. The concern of this chapter, by contrast, is with the unrestricted claim that all are.

Third, in order to establish the doctrine of unrestricted ethical relativism, three propositions would have satisfactorily to be argued for. One, that for every moral statement agreed to in this or that culture there is (or could be) a rival moral statement agreed to in some other. Two, that it could never be shown that any given moral statement is correct to the exclusion of a rival. Three, that it does not even make sense to say that a given moral statement is (or could be) correct to the exclusion of a rival.

Fourth, for those who wish to uphold the claims of unrestricted ethical cultural relativism, there are two possible lines of argument: one empirical, the other *a priori*. The empirical begins either by comparing different cultures, attempting to establish that they are at odds with one another over the entire range of their moral beliefs, or by comparing different periods of this or that same culture, and attempting to establish that the latter's moral beliefs, however fundamental, are subject to change. The *a priori* kind of argument also has two forms. In its first it endeavours to show that even if there are fundamental moral beliefs common to all men, there are still *possible* rivals to them. In its second it tries to show that moral statements are not genuine statements at all, but expressions of emotion, commands or prescriptions, neither correct therefore nor incorrect.[1] However this second form of the *a priori* argument will not require to be looked at here, since it has been countered in advance: Chapter 4 concerned itself almost wholly with establishing that moral statements are perfectly genuine from the start.

An argument in favour of moral universals and common principles

The argument most commonly advanced in favour of unrestricted ethical relativism takes the form of the first empirical argument mentioned above. Its initial premiss rests on the supposed evidence of anthropologists, sociologists, historians and the like, that different cultures have different moral beliefs even on such radical issues as killing, suicide, stealing and lying. In short, it claims that there is good evidence in support of the view that there are no moral universals, no moral beliefs which are common to all men.

From what was argued in Chapter 1, and has just been recalled, even if this complex premiss could satisfactorily be supported, *of itself* it would not establish the doctrine of extreme ethical relativism. But it cannot be supported anyway.

The argument to show that it cannot be supported needs to be spelled out at length and will take up most of what remains of this chapter. But its general drift may be outlined in advance as follows. If we wished to argue from comparative studies that groups of human beings differ in the whole range of their moral beliefs, we would need first to be confident that those whom we were comparing were in fact human. This would mean in turn that first we would have to be sure that those we were studying had the following two sets of characterising features: the possession of rationality and the possession of a minimum set of like aims (goals and aversions). But once we acknowledged that the subjects of our study possessed these characteristics, we would be constrained to acknowledge that they also possessed certain like moral principles. For all groups of beings who have these characteristics and who attempt rationally to solve the problems which arise from their having common aims, will necessarily come up with a minimum set of like beliefs concerning what is rational and irrational in their members' behaviour. For this reason men's fundamental moral beliefs, precisely because they form part of their fundamental *rational* beliefs, can no more be in conflict than can their beliefs about the fundamental logical relationships, or about the fundamental components of the world of public reference. Of necessity then we could not succeed in showing that different groups of human beings differ in all of their moral beliefs. That is the argument in skeletal form. Now to present it in detail.

I. *Men are essentially rational.* In the present context this means merely that *we would not call a group of beings 'human'* unless we had grounds for saying that they were rational.

The plausibility of this claim may be brought out in a number of ways. First, to recall some of the points that were argued in Chapter 1, we can reflect on what sort of creatures a group of beings would be that were *not* rational. *Inter alia* they would be without beliefs; without the simplest of concepts (*fish, water* and the rest); without an ability to engage in intelligent activity; without the means to make predictions or to form any systematic understanding of the world around them. Clearly they would not be men.

A simpler and perhaps more effective way of getting at man's essential rationality is to ask what is the function of rationality. The answer surely is that its function is to solve theoretical and practical problems; from which it follows that a group of beings devoid of rationality would be a group of beings unable to solve either theoretical or practical problems. They would not be men.

Further, we can reflect that typically men are language-users, and that the possession and use of language demands an already advanced degree of rationality: demands among other things the complex ability to recognise deductive and inductive relationships.

Finally, we can remind ourselves that the central question being looked at in this chapter is how men's moral beliefs compare and contrast. What is not being questioned, but is assumed from the start, is that men do have such things as moral beliefs. However, this assumption in turn presupposes that men are rational. For the having of moral beliefs demands in the first place a grasp of the ways in which men are interrelated and affect one another, and in the second place an ability consciously to act on principle.

There are, then, good conceptual reasons for holding that men are essentially rational; and, as was argued in the last chapter, conceptual reasons are neither arbitrary nor matters of 'mere convention'.

II. *Men are essentially beings that have aims.* There are many things which men aim to avoid: pains, fears, loss of freedom, thwarted expectations and so on; and many things which equally they aim to fulfil or attain: hopes, desires, pleasures, happiness.

The plausibility of this claim may be supported in much the same way as that of the first. If we had any hesitation in conceding the point, we could ask ourselves what a group of beings would be like who, while they resembled us in physical form, were altogether devoid of aims: had no desires, hopes, pleasures, pains or fears. They would not be men. For they would not, among other things, consciously engage in the activities of propagation, co-operation or communication. Indeed, given their physical vulnerability and the apparent reliance by evolution on their consciousness, their survival as individuals and as a species would never have been possible.

It might be worth interjecting here that this or that *particular* man, in the sense of this or that individual born of woman, may be devoid of rationality, or devoid of pleasures and pains. But such an individual, for both conceptual and biological reasons, is necessarily exceptional. Conceptually, man as a species must have both rationality and aims; biologically, he would not have survived without them.

III. *Some human aims are common to all men.* It is sometimes argued that all aspirations, desires, feelings and fears are dependent on and determined by the cultures in which men are reared: that no aims are given by nature. It is sometimes added that therefore men have no aims which are common to all cultures, no aims that are even *de facto* universals.

On two counts these claims are implausible. First, men constitute a single biological species, the survival of which can best and perhaps uniquely be understood on the supposition that its individuals typically share a set of fundamental goals and aversions: such goals as the desires to eat, sleep, communicate and propagate, and such aversions as the suffering of grievous pains and fears. Second, all men have a great deal of outward behaviour in common, and only the philosophical sceptic could doubt that this behaviour expresses such things as strivings, desires and fears. Everywhere men laugh, weep, embrace, look for shelter and, *above all*, speak to one another. It is implausible and perhaps even unintelligible therefore to suggest that men have no aims which are common to them all. The sceptic or anyone else who holds the contrary must accept as equally plausible that his closest friends are without fears and desires in common with the rest of men. For in both cases alike there is nothing to go on but behaviour, and that *is* common.

IV. *Because men are beings with rationality and a set of goals and aversions which are common to them all, they possess a common set of principles governing how they must behave if they are to minimise their aversions and reach the optimum number of their goals.*

The general argument to justify this final claim was presented at some length in Chapter 4, and may now be summarised as follows. Men individually have numerous aims and desires: to pursue pleasure, to avoid pain, and so on. But if these desires were satisfied without restraint, they would often bring pain, frustration and death to others. Therefore it would be irrational for any group of interacting persons not to co-operate at least negatively for the prevention or lessening of such ills. The reason for this is simply that most individuals stand to suffer more numerous and greater harms in a group or society which is without restraints than in one in which the latter are accepted and, where necessary, imposed.

At the same time, men often strongly desire goals which can be reached only by positive co-operation (as opposed to mere restraint and prevention) and in cases of this kind it would also be irrational for them not to co-operate.

What moral principles are common to all men[2]

So much for the argument in favour of there being moral principles common to all (groups of) men. We can now turn to listing these principles, and subsequently to providing justifications for them. There are eleven.

1. *Men ought not to kill others.*
2. *Men ought not to cause permanent harm of a serious nature to others.*
3. *Men ought not to torture, or otherwise inflict severe pain on others.*
4. *Men ought not seriously to deprive others of their liberties.*
5. *Men ought not seriously to deprive others of what they consider to be their more important pleasures, interests and forms of happiness, nor seriously to increase their frustrations.*

The justification of these five principles is straightforward. Typically men have a strong aversion to being killed, physically or mentally maimed, physically or mentally tortured, and deprived of what they consider to be their important pleasures, interests and forms of happiness. Given these facts, it would be irrational for any group of men not to co-operate (in the ways specified in the last chapter) for the purpose of minimising the occurrence of these ills. To put this more precisely and in the light of what has been argued before, it would be irrational of any group of men so to behave that its individual members acted in matters of killing, maiming, torturing and so on, as if the interests of other individuals were of no consequence. And given that the expression 'it is irrational for x to do (or not do) so and so' means 'x ought to do (or not do) so and so', all of this can effectively be summarised in the form of the principles listed above.

There are several points of qualification and elucidation that need to go with these principles, but since the same points will require to accompany the rest, it will be better to defer them till the list is complete.

6. *Men ought not to practise deception.*
7. *Men ought not to cheat.*
8. *Men ought not to lie.*

There are several reasons why it would be irrational for a group of men so to behave that each individual deceived, cheated and lied without consideration for the interests of others. First, lying, cheating and deceiving are often the simplest and most effective means that individuals within a group (or subsets within a group) have for doing harm to others while avoiding the consequences. These practices in other words are devices for making the inflicting of injury easier and thereby more frequent of occurrence. They are modest Gygean rings, with the power to render the doer of evil less vulnerable than he would otherwise be. At the same time they render the victim *more* vulnerable, since frequently men are led by deception or lying into situations of harm which otherwise they would not have considered entering. The second reason is that if all individuals in a group, or a significant number of individuals in a group, lied, cheated and deceived according to their several and immediate personal interests, the group would shortly be reduced to a state of debilitating discomfort and anxiety. Trust would fail, and as a result the group would be deprived both of its principal good — co-operation — and of the many benefits which the latter makes possible. Finally, there is this against lying, cheating and deception. If and when their victims become aware of them, they suffer a further injury from the very realisation that they have been deceived, cheated or lied to. Not incorrectly they feel that they have been affronted and treated with contempt.

These reasons may be summarised in the claim that the practice of lying, cheating and deception greatly increases the sum of individuals' aversions, and significantly impedes the attainment of their goals. For a group to countenance them would therefore be irrational.

Does the principle that men ought not to practise deception include that they ought not to practise *self*-deception? In other words, is it irrational for a group of men to behave in such a way that its individuals allow themselves without restraint to be deceived concerning their own other-affecting actions and activities? The answer is that it is, for the following reasons. First, and most important, self-deception enables people to do harm to others while escaping the most pervasive and effective check on harm-doing, namely conscience; the latter being effective as a moral influence because it is the rationality of the group internalised by the individual. Second, a group is in many ways less able to persuade and influence the behaviour of a self-deceiver precisely because the latter is often not aware that what he is doing is what he ought not to be doing, or because he convinces himself that for this or that reason he is justified in considering himself an exception. In short, the self-deceiver is frequently less easy to deal with than the more open and 'honest' doer of wrong. Third, for similar reasons the self-deceiver is often a poor co-operator, especially when the cost of co-operation is high. For he is able to convince himself either that he is already playing his part, or that for special reasons he is exempt from doing so. Finally, the self-deceiver in being deceived is liable to deceive others: self-deception leads on to the deception of others.

So self-deception, as it turns out, is not in the first instance a sin against the individual's 'authenticity'. Like the rest of morality, it is primarily what concerns the group or society. The authenticity of the individual is only derivatively a matter of morality.

9.   *Men ought not to break their promises.*

The reasons why men ought not to break their promises are similar to the reasons why they ought not to deceive, cheat and lie. Broken promises are frustrations of justifiable expectations. In addition they are personal affronts, they undermine trust and they destroy co-operation.

Despite its resemblance to others, the principle concerning promises needs to be treated on its own, largely because of the objection sometimes raised against it as a universal principle: that promise-keeping and promise-breaking are parts of an institution not to be found in all human groups or societies.

This objection is far from persuasive. It is true that not all societies have the institution of making formal commitments to doing things. But there are other ways of making promises than by formal commitment. It seems reasonable to argue that whenever and wherever there exists co-operation of any sort among men, by their very activity the individuals involved lead others to expect that they will carry out this or that part of their joint undertaking; what is more, they know that henceforward this will be expected of them. But all of this amounts to promise-keeping; additional and formal commitments are not required.

10.   *Men ought not to act unjustly, unfairly, with partiality.*

This principle, thanks to Aristotle, is sometimes expressed in the form: men ought not to treat equals unequally, or unequals equally. Its justification is as follows. All societies which are even moderately complex possess a number of institutions by which, or within which, certain good things and bad things have to be distributed. Families, governments, ministries, courts, companies and schools have the task of distributing goods, services, money, learning, tax-demands, fines and imprisonments. But it would be irrational for a society to make these distributions with partiality, or allow them to be made with partiality, for the following reason. The institutions in point are likely to be tolerated only if they are administered to the benefit, or to the minimum disadvantage, of all. If they are managed in such a way that they favour some to the serious disadvantage of others, these latter will not willingly co-operate in their maintenance; rather, given sufficient provocation and the right circumstances, they will do what they can to destroy them.[3]

A number of comments need to be made on this principle of justice or fairness.

(i) It is not as central as moral philosophers sometimes assert. For it is a principle which applies only to institutions, or perhaps more properly to those who represent them (judges, teachers, public servants and so on). Unlike the earlier-mentioned principles, it does not have application to all individuals (severally).

(ii) Given the shortage of goods that men need even for survival, and given the dependence everywhere of at least young children on others, there are few if any societies in which no forms of distribution are required. On the other hand, most of *our* institutions calling for distributive justice (courts, banks, examination-boards and so on) are clearly not universal.

(iii) The principle of justice stated abstractly in such forms as: Men ought not to treat individuals differently unless there are non-trivial reasons for their doing so, is often so difficult to apply that it threatens to become vacuous. For example, a just and fair distribution of educational benefits is notoriously difficult to make sense of. However determined educational administrators may be to treat equals equally, and unequals unequally, pupils are equal and unequal in so many ways that it becomes difficult, perhaps impossible, to give any determinate content to the term *equal* in the context at all. Pupils may be equal or unequal in one or more of the following (to take random examples): geographical background; social background; family background; financial background; earlier educational background; physical abilities; psychological states; potential abilities; present attainments, interests, aims, prejudices, motivations, hopes; likes and dislikes; specific gifts or lack of gifts in doing mathematics, making friends, playing cricket and getting on with teachers. What is more, similar ranges of equalities and inequalities apply to teachers, schools and the higher educational administrators themselves. Then, even on the supposition that all of this could be sorted out, the next problem to be faced is not less daunting: *How* are we to treat educational equals equally, and unequals unequally? Not to labour the point, there is no obvious answer, and the principle of impartiality in this and in similar cases is indeed recalcitrant. But, to be fair, there are other cases where its application is not baffling. For example, the equal treatment of equal shareholders is fairly straightforward, and so are the equal treatment by individual doctors of their patients and the equal treatment of defendants by their juries.

(iv) From the argument used to justify the principle of fairness or justice there emerges a way of handling the vexed question of 'rights'. Rights are not instances of peculiar properties inherent in the nature of man, nor is the notion of a 'right' irreducible. As was mentioned briefly in the last chapter, rights are simply claims or demands made by individuals on their own behalf or on behalf of others (the unborn, for example), which it would be irrational for the group or society to which they belong not to meet. To illustrate this with an example, to say that an individual has a right to be educated means that it would be irrational for society not to acknowledge his demand for education, or the demands made on his behalf. *Natural* rights are those claims which it would be irrational for men as a whole not to acknowledge. For example, to say that men have a natural right to freedom of worship means that it would be irrational for mankind as a whole so to behave that the forms of worship adopted by individuals or sets of individuals were

87

hampered or oppressed. And a similar interpretation is to be given to the expression 'natural justice'.

The moral principles so far enunciated have been negative: men ought not to kill, ought not to cheat and the rest. Are there any basic and universal positive moral principles? In other words, are there ways in which it would be irrational for a group or society not to co-operate for the attainment of positive goals or ends? Strictly speaking, for the following reason it would seem not. No society or group of men could conceivably live together in a manner describable as rational, unless there were restraints on such things as killing, torturing and depriving others of their liberty. But a group of men could quite rationally live together without co-operating towards the achievement of any positive goods. They might simply prefer it that way.

Thus the best that can be done by way of introducing a positive moral principle is to say the following. If and when a significant number of individuals in a group have a set of like and highly valued positive goals which can be attained only by co-operation, and there are no overriding considerations against co-operation, it would be irrational for those individuals not to co-operate. Put more briefly this may be worded as follows:

11.   *Men ought to co-operate for the attainment of their overriding goals.*

It is not possible to cash this principle in a series of such lower-level statements as: men ought to provide others with pleasure, ought to further the truth among their fellows, ought to seek the happiness of others. For, as has already been said, it would not be irrational for a group of men to desire only those pleasures and forms of happiness which each could attain by his unaided efforts.

However, having conceded this much, we are entitled to add that usually men in groups do have positive like goals of the sort that can be attained only by co-operation. Usually then, in most groups and societies, there are forms of co-operation towards positive goals that it would be irrational not to engage in. Education will serve as an example. Given the strong desire that individuals in societies such as ours have for education, whether as a means to further ends or as an end in itself, it would plainly be irrational for us not to co-operate for the provision of that education. It is this in fact which supports the truth of the statement that, in our society at least, all men have a *right* to education. That right may or may not be God-given: it *is* given by reason.

This completes the task of listing the moral principles. A number of general comments on them need now to be appended.

(i) The aversions which form the springboard of the negative moral principles are only *prima facie* aversions. By this is meant that men will rationally avoid being killed, tortured or whatever, provided that more important considerations do not supervene. Thus, for example, while men have an aversion to being killed, they will often prefer the latter to bringing harm to their country or to their friends.

Because of this, the moral principles themselves are not absolute but *prima facie* in force. For example, men ought not to kill, torture or lie unless there are overriding considerations to justify their doing so. One *may* kill or lie in self-defence. One *may* break a promise to avert still greater harm.

(ii) The claim that men have *prima facie* aversions to being killed, tortured and so on, is not meant as an empirical generalisation. Rather, what is meant is that if a group of beings existed who did not have aversions to being killed, maimed and the rest, they could not conceivably count as men. They could not even count as living organisms, since their manner of surviving – if they survived at all – would certainly not be that of typical complex organisms.

(iii) The division of moral principles into eleven, and only eleven, is not a matter of necessity. Some moral philosophers prefer to group maiming and torture under the single description of 'inflicting grievous physical or mental harm'. Others prefer to treat promise-breaking as basically the same as lying. And so on.

Even so, there *are* reasons for keeping the eleven separate. It can be pointed out, for example, that maiming is markedly different from torture in that it brings about *permanent* serious harm, or that promise-breaking is different from lying in that it does not of itself involve the intention to deceive. But in the end it should be conceded that little of substance hangs on which divisions are adhered to. Nothing will alter the fact that men ought not to torture and maim; or that they ought not to break their promises and lie.

(iv) The final principle, stating that men ought to co-operate for the attainment of their overriding positive goals may seem to some to bring too many activities within the scope of morality. It might be objected, for example, that to make the provision of secondary and tertiary education a matter of moral obligation is, to say the least, untraditional.

However, to this it may be replied that the provision of secondary and tertiary education in societies like ours is not a *separate* sort of moral obligation. It is an application to our own circumstances of the principle which in the end constitutes the whole of morality: that men's aversions should be minimised and the optimum number of their goals achieved. Whenever the aversions and goals in question are weighty enough to support the conclusion that it would be irrational not to take action respecting them, it seems reasonable to bring them within the scope of morality.

Cultural relativism and morality

We come now to the doctrine of ethical relativism. Is morality *in toto* culturally relative? Are its basic principles culturally relative? Are all or at least some of its lower-level judgments culturally relative?

From everything that has been said it is clear that morality *in toto*, the whole venture of morality, is not culturally relative; for no group or society could conceivably be without it. This follows from the fact that morality is nothing other than rationality applied to men's goals and aversions, and that the possession of these latter is essential to man's nature: is part of what for fundamental conceptual reasons we cannot *help* but attribute to man.

The basic principles of morality likewise are not culturally relative, since they result from the application of common human rationality to the set of aversions which also are common to men, and (in the case of the last principle) to the fact that men are prone to those sorts of overriding desires which demand co-operation for their fulfilment.

Like the first, this point demands no further elucidation, since the whole of the present chapter has been concerned to show that the basic principles of morality are derived from what is common to men. However, it may be worth adding that while no group or society can behave over long periods in defiance of the *entire* set of basic moral principles, given groups, societies or cultures can and often do exhibit considerable amounts of immoral behaviour; just as some people, while possessing the principle of contradiction, manage to talk a great deal of inconsistent nonsense. But if talking nonsense here and there or in bouts does not argue for the relativity of the principles of logic, behaving immorally here and there or in bouts should not be thought to argue for the relativity of the principles of morality.

Lower-level moral judgments are simply applications of one or more of the basic moral principles to special sets of circumstances or conditions, and since most of these basic principles are concerned with aversions which are *common* to men, the lower-level judgments generated concerning them are no more culturally relative than the moral principles themselves. An example will help here. Some societies (but only some) possess the institution which we call marriage. In some of these societies (but again only some) there is the additional practice according to which partners entering into marriage make explicit promises of conjugal fidelity. The moral judgment that in such (promise-making) institutions men ought not to commit adultery is not a culturally relative judgment. It is merely an instance of the universal moral truth or principle that men in *all* groups or societies ought not to break their promises. This moral judgment, it needs to be stressed, is not, and does not entail, that all societies ought to have the institution of marriage, nor that in all societies married persons ought to promise fidelity. It is simply that *if* a society has the institution of marriage and *if* in addition it has the practice according to which promises of fidelity are made in marriage, then in *these* circumstances men ought not to commit adultery.

While most of the moral principles are concerned with common aversions, there are two (5, 11) which allow for the fact that some aversions and goals may be peculiar to this or that sort of society. This is important for the following reason. It has been argued, both in the present and in the last chapter, that at bottom morality rests on the principle that any given group or society ought to minimise its aversions and realise the optimum number of its goals. But from this it follows that if there are societies possessing *conflicting* sets of aversions or goals, these societies may arrive at equally conflicting moral judgments. And provided that the possession of the aversions or goals in question does not rest on, or derive from, ignorance or irrational belief (since morality is fundamentally a rational affair), not only is there no method for settling which of the conflicting judgments is uniquely correct, but it would not even make sense to say that one of them is uniquely correct. Therefore, insofar as they may be said to be true at all, each of the conflicting judgments is true relative to its own group or culture.

This may seem a major concession to ethical cultural relativism. In reality it is but small. For we do not have the means of making sure *a priori* that this or that conflict is not due merely to ignorance or false belief. By contrast we are sure from experience that numerous conflicts considered at one time to be without solution have subsequently been settled thanks to the acquisition of new information.

Nonetheless, it must be conceded that there are in theory cases of conflicting lower-level moral judgments which will always remain beyond solution; and these are best described as culturally relative. An example again will help to bring out the point. Let us consider two societies, A and B. In A men have strong aversions to seeing pain inflicted on animals, and take considerable pleasure in seeing the latter protected and otherwise cared for. In B men have no such aversions and no such pleasures. Let us suppose further (the part that would be difficult to establish) that the men of both societies hold the same sets of beliefs and have the same sorts of appreciations concerning the nature of animals (that they are conscious, that they feel pain, distress and pleasure), and that neither society holds or is influenced by ill-supported, inconsistent, or plainly false beliefs. Given all this, society A may reasonably make the moral judgment that pain ought not to be inflicted on animals. Society B may quite as reasonably deny this, and continue to approve of pain-inflicting pursuits even as sports. In this case it would make no sense to say that one of the conflicting judgments is uniquely correct. (Other examples could easily be constructed around such moral judgments as: men ought never to engage in warfare; men ought to be punished for their wrong-doings whatever the consequences of the punishment, good or bad.)

To summarise and bring this section to a close, there is no case for ethical cultural relativism in what concerns morality as a whole, nor in what concerns the basic principles of morality; nor again in what concerns those lower-level moral judgments which have still to do with goals and aversions common to men. In what concerns the remaining moral judgments, the following is to be said. Where conflicts exist there is a *prima facie* case for relativism. But there will always be enormous difficulty in establishing that this or that conflict does not derive from ignorance or irrational belief.

Two remaining arguments concerning ethical cultural relativism

At the beginning of this chapter it was said that there are two lines of argument open to those who might wish to uphold the claims of ethical cultural relativism: one empirical, the other *a priori*. The first and more important form of the empirical argument has now been examined carefully, while the second form of the *a priori* argument, as was pointed out earlier, was met in advance in Chapter 4. There remains to be looked at, then, the second form of the empirical argument, the one attempting to show that radical changes have occurred within this or that culture, and the first form of the *a priori* argument, the one attempting to establish that even if there are sets of moral beliefs common to men, there are also possible sets to rival them. These arguments will need to be met only in outline here, since they are similar to those presented and rebutted in Chapter 1.

To begin with the reply to the second form of the empirical argument. There is and could be no empirical evidence supporting the claim that men in this or that culture are in the process of radically changing their moral beliefs or have so changed them. For there are tight conceptual constraints on the sorts of changes that men can carry through. The concept of man — a concept which, it has been argued, is not the result of idle choice — is of a being who is rational and subject to death, pain, joy and pleasure. But as long as men continue to be of this kind they will, for the reasons developed in the first part of this chapter, continue to have the selfsame set of moral principles as they have always had. For example, as long as men continue to die and continue individually to dislike death, it will be irrational for any society to behave in such a way that its individuals may kill as and when its suits their several and selfish interests.

But surely, it might be urged, the human species *could* change radically in the future. Surely men *could* become immortal, beyond pain and devoid of aims.

It is by no means clear that they could, nor even that this suggestion is intelligible. For in such supposed circumstances the human species would be replaced not so much by another species as by another genus altogether. More important, even if these speculations are intelligible, no conclusions may justifiably be drawn from them concerning what *at present* we are entitled to count as moral or immoral. For the limits of what we may count as moral or immoral are determined by the limits of the concept of man which at present we are constrained to work with: the concept of a rational animal.

The same sorts of remarks are to be made concerning that form of the *a priori* argument which would attempt to establish that the basic moral principles do not constitute a *unique* set, and are therefore subject to replacement. As to man's rational principles, it was argued in detail in Chapter 1 that these could not be replaced, either at once or piecemeal. As to the other side of man's nature, his possession of basic goals and aversions, it has been argued also that no changes in this could occur either; not at any rate without producing an all-embracing collapse of our understanding.

What is certain then is this. In any discussion concerning human cultures and their moral beliefs, there is no escape from the limits of our present concept of man; and within those limits most of our present moral thinking is secure.

FURTHER READING

*Bambrough, R. "Proof of the Objectivity of Morals", *Situationism and the New Morality*, R.L. Cunningham (ed.), New York, 1970.

*Benedict, R. *Patterns of Culture*, Boston, 1934.

Brandt, R. *Hopi Ethics,* Chicago, 1954.

*Brennan, J.G. *Ethics and Morals*, New York, 1973, Chap. 2.

Coburn, R. "Relativism and the Basis of Morality", *Philosophical Review*, 85 (1976), pp. 87-93.

*Downie, R.S. *Roles and Values*, London, 1971, Chap. 8.

Darwall, S.L. "Human and Moral Relativism", *Personalist*, 58 (1977), pp. 199-207.

Edel, A. "On a Certain Value-dimension in Analyses of Moral Relativism", *The Journal of Philosophy,* 67 (1970), pp. 584-588.

Foot, P. "Moral Beliefs", *Theories of Ethics*, Oxford, 1967.

Harman, G. "Moral Relativism Defended", *Philosophical Review,* 84 (1975), pp. 3-22.

Jensen, H. "Gilbert Harman's Defence of Moral Relativism", *Philosophical Studies,* 30 (1976), pp. 401-407.

Kolnai, A. "Moral Consensus", *Proceedings of the Aristotelian Society*, 70 (1969-70), pp. 93-118.

Lean, M. "Aren't Moral Judgments 'Factual'?", *The Personalist,* 51 (1970), pp. 259-285.

*Lukes, S. "Relativism: Cognitive and Moral", *The Aristotelian Society*, supp. vol. 48 (1974), pp. 165-189.

Monro, D.H. *Empiricism and Ethics*, Cambridge, 1967.

Nielsen, K. "Ethical Relativism and the Facts of Cultural Relativity", *Social Research*, 33 (1966), pp. 531-551.

Nielsen, K. "Anthropology and Ethics", *Journal of Value Inquiry*, 5 (1971), pp. 253-266.

Phillips, D.Z. & Mounce, H.O. *Moral Practices,* London, 1969.

Pratte, H.E. "Moral Questions in the Context of Today's Rapidly Changing Society", *Journal of Thought*, 5 (1970), pp. 254-261.

Reid, C.L. "Popular Subjectivism and Relativism", *Journal of Critical Analysis,* 2 no. 3 (1970), pp. 36-42.

Ruben, D.H. "Social Relativism and the Theory of Right", *Analysis*, 34 (1974), pp. 167-173.

Runciman, W.G. "Relativism: Cognitive and Moral", *The Aristotelian Society*, supp. vol. 48 (1974), pp. 191-208.

*Stace, W.T. "Ethical Relativism", *Philosophy and Contemporary Issues,* J. Burr & M. Goldinger (eds), New York, 1972.

Sumner, C.G. *Folkways*, Boston, 1906.

Taylor, P. "Social Science and Ethical Relativism", *Journal of Philosophy,* 55 (1958), pp. 32-44.

Turnbull, C.M. *The Mountain People,* New York, 1972.

Wellman, C.P. "Ethical Disagreement and Objective Truth", *American Philosophical Quarterly,* 12 (1975), pp. 211-221.

Westermarck, E.A. *The Origin and Development of Moral Ideas,* 2 vols., New York, 1906-8.

*Williams, B. *Morality,* Harmondsworth, 1972.

Williams, B. "The Truth in Relativism", *Proceedings of the Aristotelian Society,* 75 (1974-5), pp. 215-228.

CHAPTER 6
THE CURRICULUM

The purpose of this book has not been to pursue the problem of cultural relativism in a philosophically disinterested way, but to examine it in relation to the current debate concerning what teachers ought, or even have the right to teach. For, as was mentioned in the Introduction, while the traditional view of knowledge which children are encouraged to acquire in school is that it is both worthwhile and objective, recent educationists like M. Young and his colleagues have advanced the view that what counts as knowledge in schools is not objective at all, but is what middle-class teachers and others have decided will count as knowledge. More widely, they have claimed that no knowledge is more than what power-groups in this or that society wish to be counted as such.

In the preceding chapters it has been argued that knowledge is not relative to classes or any other sub-groups in society, at least in its principal areas — in the natural sciences, the social sciences, commonsense and morality. But the discussion needs to go further. For it has been claimed by the educationists mentioned above that the school curriculum *as a whole* lacks objective foundations and is necessarily the expression of class or some other power-grouping. Because of this, the present chapter will look at the problem of the curriculum in general, and will undertake the following tasks. It will argue that the principles on which a school curriculum can and should be established are not expressions of class or any sort of grouping in society. It will argue that a fairly detailed outline of what should be taught in schools can be derived from common human principles, even if Western democratic values are needed to justify the extension of it to each and every individual. Finally, it will examine explicitly the question of cultural relativism and the curriculum, and will show that neither the cognitive content of the latter nor the choice of that content is culturally relative.

The general method to be followed

Philosophers and others who from time to time have tackled the problem of the curriculum have done so in a variety of ways. Some have appealed to intuition, others to metaphysical analysis, others to the nature of knowledge, others again to human nature and to its supposedly spontaneous growth and development. The method to be employed here will be the same as that used in earlier chapters (particularly 2, 3 and 4). It was argued there, among other things, that philosophy is not discontinuous with the rest of men's forms of enquiry, and that philosophers like all of us are concerned to advance hypotheses and theories in an effort to make sense of their data (experiences, beliefs and so on), if and when these are puzzling: that is, if and when they appear to lack unity and continuity with already established beliefs and patterns of thought. Thus, to take examples, in order to make sense of this or that set of data, philosophers have on occasion hypothesised that there are such things as universals, numbers or classes; or that the physical world alone possesses genuine reality. In keeping with this method, in Chapter 4 the hypothesis was put forward that the concept of 'ought' is best analysed in terms of 'aims' and 'reasons', and that as a result morality should be seen as an application of rationality to men's other-affecting behaviour.

The theory to be put forward and defended in this chapter is similar to the above, and may be summarised in the following three claims. First, when we ask what the curriculum in schools should be, we are properly interpreted as asking what sort of curriculum can be *rationally justified*. Second, the notion of a rational justification is best explicated in terms of aims and reasons. Third, what in general the activities and pursuits of schools should be is what their respective societies would be irrational not to foster or if necessary enforce, and in addition (though more moderately) what these societies have some good grounds positively to encourage or at least to allow.

Some preliminary points

Before the central issues of the curriculum can intelligibly be discussed, a number of preliminary points need to be made.

First, what from now on will be understood by the word 'curriculum' is the sum total of the learning activities which go on in schools (or other educational institutions) and have been planned precisely as learning activities, or at least are intended as such. It does not include such things as the fights and feuds that occur in the playground or staffroom, but it does embrace things like talks given by fire-prevention officers, or mock interviews with supposed employers. The curriculum then is wider than the contents of books and the words of teachers, but not as wide as all that goes on in schools.

Second, there is no one whose expertise can justify the claim that his specialist knowledge alone can settle what the curriculum should be. This is a point which will be argued more fully later, since it is not uncontested: that is, there are educationists and others who do lay claim to such expertise, if not for themselves at least on behalf of others.

As a first go off it might be objected here that those who think systematically about the curriculum, as educationists and some philosophers do, are for that very reason entitled to be considered its experts. But this is not so;

or at any rate to make use of the terminology of expertise in this way is misleading. It is liable to suggest, and clearly has suggested to some, that there are experts to tell us what are to be the components of the curriculum, in the way that there are experts to tell us what should be the components of a superjet or submarine. There are no experts of this kind.

Third, while it is possible in this way — that is, without possessing narrowly specialist expertise — to say in general what the contents of a school's curriculum should be, the putting into effect of that curriculum depends on many facts and circumstances which plainly do fall within the province of experts. It depends, for example, on the cognitive development of pupils; on the ability and training of teachers; on the nature and structure of subjects studied; on the design of schools and school facilities; on the psychological and social attitudes of pupils, parents and local communities; on the pressures exerted by such bodies as political parties, churches and teachers' federations. These and a host of other things influence and help to determine what is possible or suitable in a given school, and clearly most of them require the scrutiny and advice of such experts as psychologists, subject-specialists or administrators.

Fourth, to have a curriculum theory is not an intellectual luxury, something that can and perhaps ought to be dispensed with. For, as will become clearer in the course of this chapter, every teacher's practice presupposes and is embedded in a background theory, and whoever finally decides what is to go on in schools willy-nilly makes a set of assumptions. But surely it is important to unearth these assumptions, particularly when, in periods like our own, extreme and incompatible claims concerning the curriculum are to be heard. It is claimed by some, for example, that children's activities should be chosen and organised solely by the classroom teacher; by others on the contrary that not teachers but governments should control the detail of what children do and learn. On a related issue it is argued by some that all curricula are at present in need of radical revision, on the alleged grounds that what now is done is the result for the most part of the imposition of middle-class preferences. By others it is still more starkly proposed that children would be better off without schools altogether. In this climate of conflicting opinion it is unreasonable to suggest that theoretical considerations concerning the curriculum are unnecessary, or that the teaching profession should give its undivided attention to practical issues. In fact it could be argued that the most practical thing to be done at the moment is precisely to make teachers reflect on what they ought to be doing; since few things undermine their confidence so deeply as doubts and anxieties concerning the purpose of their whole enterprise.

The parallel with moral theory

It was brought out in Chapter 4 that the concept of practical rationality — the

97

concept concerned with the having and giving of reasons for pursuing some things and avoiding others — forms part of a body of concepts which are so fundamental to our ways of making sense of experience that without them we would have little left of human thought at all. In the same context it was further argued that what is practically rational for a group, culture or society to do, is what favours that group's ends or goals, and what promises to lessen its aversions; to go further, that it is *irrational* for a group not to do these things if at the same time there are no clearly better reasons against them. Finally, the important distinction was made between principles common to all men as rational beings and applications of those principles to institutions peculiar only to some. By way of illustration it was pointed out that while the institution of monogamous marriage is not common to all, men's moral behaviour within that institution where it does exist is governed by principles that are.

This analysis of practical rationality may now be given application along the following lines to the problem of the curriculum. Just as societies typically have certain aims (goals and aversions) as a result of which it is irrational for them not to require certain sorts of other-affecting behaviour of their members, so they typically have aims as a result of which it is irrational for them not to initiate, foster and even enforce certain activities designed to bring about learning, and as a result of which also it is rational for them to encourage other activities of the kind. And, as in the case of morality, the important distinction holds between principles on the one hand and application of those principles to peculiar institutions and circumstances on the other.

Common human aims having educational implications

In the course of the discussion on morality there was drawn up a list of goals and aversions typical of men: it was asserted, for example, that men typically have aversions to being killed, maimed, tortured and lied to. The point of adding the word 'typically' was to make provision for exceptions. To illustrate this point, if some people commit suicide by starving themselves to death, this does nothing to lessen the truth of the claim that men *typically* wish to eat or wish to preserve their lives.

If, to go back for a moment, we ask how it is possible for us to establish these sorts of claims about men's typical goals and aversions, the answer is that in attempting to do so we are able to rely on a number of things. We have, to start with, an intuitive grasp of our own fundamental goals and aversions, and we know from our close acquaintance with friends and others that these aims are not peculiar to ourselves as individuals. Then, not implausibly we go on to interpret them more widely as typical of men in general, on the grounds *inter alia* that they are closely linked to such biological functions as the survival of individuals, of societies, and in the end of the whole human species. In other words, our opinion of the human typicality of these aims fits in with our biological beliefs and theories. But that is not all. Our opinion is further and amply supported by the study of such things as history, literature and anthropology. For the striking conclusion to be drawn from these is that there are very few exceptions, if indeed there are any at all, to the claim that men have aversions of the sort referred to above. Yet again, in recent years human nature has found something of a forum in the United Nations, and we find the same set of fundamental aims repeated and underlined in the latter's documents; particularly in its charter and in the reports, declarations and accounts of its committees, commissions and subsidiary organisations.

The relevance of all this to the question of the curriculum is that there is a further set of well attested aims typical of human groups or societies which, while not in themselves describable as educational, nonetheless carry educational implications. These aims are of a kind which all societies typically pursue on behalf of their members *conjointly*, but not severally: in other words, on behalf of themselves as societies. To illustrate the distinction at issue here: societies typically have their survival as an aim, but it does not follow from this that they have the survival of each and every of their members as an aim. Some do: some do not.

Aims which are typical of all societies and carry educational implications

These further aims typical of any human society may be listed as follows:
1. *The moral behaviour of that society's own members; and whatever understanding and training are needed for the acquisition and stabilising of that behaviour.*
This follows directly from what was argued in Chapters 4 and 5: namely, that moral behaviour is that other-affecting conduct which a society would be irrational not to desire and demand of its members; and, given this, it would further be irrational of a society not to take the educational means necessary to achieve such behaviour.
2. *The health and general physical well-being of the society's members: at least the minimum required for the attaining of its other goals and the avoidance of its aversions.*
3. *Such material goods as food and shelter for its members; again at least enough to avert the sorts of disorders which arise from severe want (theft, violence and the like).*
4. *A level of contentedness among its members, sufficient to prevent the social ills likely to arise from widespread disquiet.*
5. *The transmission of whatever available knowledge, skills and techniques are required for the solving of its pressing problems and the meeting of its pressing needs.*

6.   *The maintenance of a socio-political structure, organisation and har-mony, sufficient to avoid calamitous divisions among its members.*
7.   *Security from outside attack and other forms of serious interference, and whatever means are needed to provide that security.*

From these and perhaps other fundamental aims which are clearly typical of human societies, it would be possible straight away to begin drawing educational and curricular conclusions. But these latter would have to be of a fairly general kind, and since one of the purposes of this chapter is to put together some specific remarks on the curriculum in countries like England or Australia, it will be more profitable to proceed at this point by adding to the above list such further aims as characterise Western liberal democracies; and then to go on to argue for a curriculum on the basis of the twin set of aims — those typical of all societies and those typical of our kinds of democracy. It can be left till later to see what implications the existence of such a double set of aims has for the problem of cultural relativism.

There are very great differences *in fact* between Western liberal democracies and most other countries, since the former are wealthy, developed and technically well organised, and these differences quite properly exert a wide influence on their schools' curricula. But what is at stake here is a set of more fundamental differences, partly resulting from and partly constitutive of their being democracies of a certain kind in the first place. These differences, amounting to a set of aims typical of Western liberal democracies, and due largely to the high value they put on *individuals*, are concerned this time not with what typically a society wants for its corporate good, but what it wants for the good of its members severally. Finally, all of the aims concern not necessarily the direct and positive provision of this or that set of goods, but the ensuring of *equal access* to, or *opportunity of attaining* them.

Aims characteristic of Western liberal democracies

These aims are the following:
1.   *A basic standard of health and general bodily well-being for each member.*
2.   *A reasonable level of material well-being for each member: at least sufficient to constitute freedom from serious want in respect of food, clothing and shelter.*
3.   *A corresponding level of personal well-being: that is, a reasonable degree of such things as self-confidence, independence of character, happiness and inner contentment.*
4.   *Individual interest, satisfaction and self-fulfilment through the development of talents and related abilities.*
5.   *The development of skills, qualities and whatever else is needed for the choosing and pursuit of an individual's way of life, job, career, interests and so on.*

100

6.   *A reasonable level of social well-being; that is, the possession of such things as ease and ability in getting on with one's immediate acquaintances and in adapting to a wider community.*
7.   *A voice and active participation in the social and democratic organisation of the different levels of society: including such things as the freedom to associate with others; to express opinions and to criticise; to vote; to form and work for political parties.*
8.   *Tolerance on the part of all individuals, in order to ensure the rights and freedoms of others.*

It is important to stress the following points concerning these aims.

They are typical, and therefore allow of exceptions. They are characteristic of our societies only in general, not of each and every sub-group within them. They are no more than aims, and therefore may not have been, or some of them may not have been, fully achieved. They are aims which often have to be weighed against each other, or weighed against those which societies pursue with an eye on their *corporate* good. (Because of this, the importance and emphasis given to a particular aim will often vary with circumstances. A threat to the corporate existence of a society, for example, often leads rapidly to the curtailment of individual liberties, or choice of employment.) Finally, and notoriously, the existence of this set of aims, like the existence of the first, does not at once dictate the nature of the most suitable means of achieving them.

The curriculum that follows from the above aims

With the two sets of aims before us, a curriculum will now be argued for – or, more properly, a *curriculum-content* will be argued for. No attempt will be made to deal with such questions as how long children should remain at school; at what stages they should be taught this or that; how much arithmetic, say, they should do by comparison with other studies; whether or not they should be taught in open-plan schools or with integrated programmes of learning; what methods teachers would best be advised to adopt; at what point, if any, pupils should begin to pursue their specialist interests. Further, what will be argued for will be the typical school curriculum, and therefore nothing will be said concerning the needs of special groups of children – of the physically or mentally handicapped, of the peculiarly gifted or of the totally recalcitrant.[1]

(1) *Basic skills*

All children, given the ability, should acquire the basic skills of reading, writing, handling of vocabulary and expressing themselves with reasonable articulateness; and the fact that teaching and training in these skills is rationally and fully justified is not hard to see.

101

To begin with, competence in them is necessary for the carrying out of a host of very ordinary but important undertakings; such as: shopping (where increasingly the reading of labels on goods is needed); reading road signs and names of streets; filling in forms; reading newspapers; following knitting-patterns or recipes for cooking; writing to friends, insurance companies or bureaucratic bodies; taking however modest a part in the processes of democracy. No doubt it would be possible at a pinch to get by without doing any of these things; but it follows from the principal aims characteristic of Western liberal democracies that children should be enabled to *choose for themselves* whether or not to get by without them. They should not be deprived of that choice in the name of educational theories holding that all is well so long as children are having subjectively satisfying experiences, or that competence in the basic skills is alien to their working-class or some other culture.

Second, a person unable to read is for the most part confined within a much narrower compass of views, theories and beliefs than are open to the reader. It is true that in this respect radio and television have considerably lessened the importance of the written word, but they are far from having undermined it altogether. The vast body of literature that constitutes the human corpus of thought, fancy and learning is not in fact available through radio, television or even tape-recordings, and it is not likely to be within the conjecturable future. More important, reading is still both the cheaper and more effective way of assimilating and concentrating on many expressed forms of thought, and it may well turn out even in the long run that in the study of such subjects as mathematics, physics, logic and economics it will not be possible to make much progress without the ability to read. It is worth adding that even if such things as tapes were to replace the written word altogether, there is no reason to believe that the teaching of the comprehension, assimilation and vocabulary required for the use of those tapes would be any easier than the teaching of reading and writing. One suspects that in many subject-areas it would be harder.

Third, reading, writing and a good grasp of language are needed for the pursuit of most careers that are rewarding (in all senses of that word), and as a result of this a child who is without such skills can have very little say in what he or she will do in later life. But one of the principal aims of societies like ours, as was seen, is precisely to provide all children with access to a reasonable range of opportunities, and — within the limits of their capacities — to enable them to choose for themselves the direction of their future lives. Because of this, it would be irrational of our societies not to provide them with the basically necessary skills, and not to insist in the strongest manner possible that schools should take the teaching of these skills seriously.

Fourth, if the teaching of these skills is important for ensuring that society's individual members have each a tolerable range of choices in the sorts of jobs they might do, it is also important for ensuring that society as a body has the kinds of experts it needs for the fulfilment of its other aims — such experts as doctors, physicists, lawyers or engineers. In other words, the importance of the teaching of the basic skills rests as much on aims belonging to the first set, as on aims belonging to the second. The difference is that aims of the first kind do not entail that the basic skills should be imparted to each and every child.

Fifth, a person without the ability to read is on two counts without one of men's greatest sources of interest. For reading is an *immediate* source to those who enjoy flights of fancy, drama, poetry or the study of nature and man; and it provides an *indirect* source for those who make use of it in the pursuit of hobbies, handyman skills, car maintenance, first aid and countless other things. Of course no one doubts the possibility of leading an interesting life without the help of reading; but at the same time no one can fairly doubt that the ability to read has enabled most people to pursue more interesting activities than they would otherwise have found possible.

The sixth and last argument is a highly general one, summarising most of what might be said on the subject. It is that the basic skills discussed in this section are essential, or near-essential, to *all* of the physical, material, personal, social and political well-being of such complex and developed societies as our own. The attaining and maintaining of health, security, freedom, understanding, tolerance and adaptation to change, together with all the other of our corporate and individual goals, depend on effective communication; and this in turn depends on the skills of reading, writing, grasp of vocabulary and articulate expression. Unless we could altogether turn the clock back, we would be useless without them.

One last point here. Not a great deal of emphasis so far has been given to the skills associated with the use and understanding of the spoken word. However, it should be obvious that those who are not able easily to understand what others say, or to express themselves with clarity and fluency, are at a still greater disadvantage than those who cannot read or write. This is because most of our face-to-face exchanges of information are effected through the spoken word, and again many if not most of the interesting jobs in society depend upon it. Politicians, doctors, television personalities, lawyers, teachers and all engaged in close and immediate relations with others, need to be fully articulate. Employers in commerce and industry are frequently heard to remark that applicants for the jobs which they have to offer are surprisingly poor in the skills of oral communication. On the assumption that this is true, their remarks should not be ignored. For it is not rational to teach children in such a way that they (or some of them) are kept from succeeding in life because they lack ability and ease in face-to-face communication.

(2) *Moral training and education*

It is sometimes objected from the start that moral training and education is not in any way the concern of the schools, and that the latter should keep to their more acknowledged tasks of teaching such subjects as spelling and mathematics. But it can be seen at once from the arguments of Chapters 4 and 5 that this is wrong. A society would be irrational not to take the steps that are needed to ensure some level of moral behaviour among its members, and in our kinds of society schools are still the most important means of making a substantial and organised effort at taking such steps. Moral training and education in schools, therefore, are as justified as the teaching of basic skills.

A second and more specific objection raised is that where moral training and education are attempted, teachers usually turn out to be doing no more than imposing their own largely middle-class values upon their pupils. Moral training and education therefore, it is concluded, either should not be part of a school's curriculum at all, or at the most they should constitute an attempt to foster and develop the pupil's own values or those of his or her class. This sort of objection however is not very compelling since, to refer again to Chapters 4 and 5, insofar as teachers impose upon others the values which belong narrowly to their own social class, they are not engaged in moral education at all. Morality correctly understood is not the affair of this or that peculiar group or groups, but is the expression of what is rational in respect of conduct for any given society as a whole.

It is important to bear in mind that teachers in schools have three quite different tasks to carry out in what concerns morality. First, they must aim at instilling habits of moral behaviour in their pupils; even if for the time being the latter do not see the point and reasonableness of those habits. Second, from the fact that moral conduct is rational conduct, it follows that as soon as children are able to grasp and make sense of the issues involved, teachers should make every effort to get them to see for themselves the reasonableness of moral behaviour. Third, like society as a whole, teachers must impose and enforce moral behaviour if and when the need arises and they feel able to do so. That is, independently of their aim to bring about both moral habits in their pupils' behaviour and rational conviction in their minds, there are occasions when teachers *prima facie* have a plain duty to intervene and simply to stop what is going on. For example, if some children in a school are severely bullied and tormented by others, and there is a hope of putting an end to such occurrences without making matters worse, teachers clearly must attempt to do so, and society should require them to.

Some of this may sound alarming, appearing to make teachers into moral busybodies or even bullies themselves. But it should be remembered that what so far has been at stake is the training, educating and on occasion obliging of children not to kill, torture, bully, cheat, lie, or do anything else seriously to violate the principles set down in Chapter 5. The undertaking of such tasks as these surely is not alarming. Further, there has been no suggestion that in the carrying out of these tasks teachers should not take into account that there is considerable uncertainty over this or that application of the moral principles referred to. Rationality itself demands that they should, and a major part of moral education consists precisely in getting pupils both to see the difference between principles and their applications, and to acquire some skill in weighing arguments for and against those of the latter which are seriously held to be in doubt.

It can in fact plausibly be argued that in the present period of the development of Western liberal societies, moral education is more important than it has been in most periods past: on the grounds that given the weakening of such external authorities as the churches, it is becoming increasingly necessary that as children grow up they understand the reasons behind society's moral imperatives. Further, many changes have occurred and are occurring as a result of scientific innovation, which require a great deal of thought and argument before men can hope to discern which are the correct or best applications to them of the fundamental moral principles. Examples of such changes are those ensuing upon the development of nuclear weapons, contraceptives, rapid communications, prolongation of life, overpopulation, and transplantation of limbs. The likelihood moreover is that even greater changes, and in more rapid succession, are yet to come.

(3) *Development in character and personal relations*

Some of the schools which are now referred to rather contemptuously as 'old-fashioned' considered the personal development of their pupils to be a major part of their concern. In recent years by contrast attempts at this kind of development have been looked upon as beyond the business of the schools, or as a piece of paternalism, interference and oppression on the part of middle-class teachers.

The latter views are mistaken. One of the fundamental aims of Western liberal societies is that their members individually should lead reasonably contented and happy lives; and given that success in the development of personal qualities and the handling of relations with others is at least as important in the fulfilment of that aim as the acquisition of skills, interests and learning, schools ought to play a part in contributing to that success. The only room for discussion would seem to be over the possibility and effectiveness of this or that means, not over the end itself.

To forestall one kind of objection, it should be said that this part of the curriculum need not and should not be made up of time-consuming periods with talks on how to be happy or on how to get on with others. It should mainly consist instead of such things as the way in which the school itself is run, in good relations both among members of staff and between the latter and their pupils, and in remarks, hints and expressions of encouragement here and there in the classroom, at games or at recreation. In the later stages of schooling, personal development and relations with others will naturally become the subject of more extended discussion, both formal and informal; but this again need not be more than incidental to other activities and studies.

The place and importance given to personal happiness and fulfilment here should not be misunderstood. Teachers have sometimes interpreted their task in the matter as no more than that of ensuring present subjective states and feelings of happiness in their pupils, and have taken these to be the principal if not the sole criterion of their success in teaching. What instead is at issue, and in accord with the relevant fundamental aims of Western liberal societies, is the fulfilment and happiness of children not only in their present state as children but as adults-to-be. The development of their character, therefore, and their ability to enter into successful relations with others should correspondingly be carried out as much with an eye to the future as to the present.

(4) *Training and education in health and physical well-being*

Little needs to be said to justify the place of physical and health training and education in a school's curriculum, since it follows fairly directly from the aim common to all societies for the collective health and physical well-being of their members, and from the desire common to Western liberal societies for the health and physical well-being of each and every of their members. There is a great deal of discussion, and merited discussion, over exactly what and how much should be done and by what means; but here the point is simply to establish that something should be done at all.

(5) *Mathematics*

Given what has been said so far concerning the basic skills and other components, it is not difficult to see that, and why, mathematics should form part of the typical curriculum. To begin with, some knowledge of it is needed for the carrying out of quite fundamental tasks: such as shopping, simple budgeting and other handling of money, measuring for dressmaking, or calculating the right quantities of paint and wallpaper for decorating a room. Second, mathematics is incontestably the key to many of the major works which our societies want carried out — in engineering, physics, accounting, medicine, banking and many other areas besides. For this reason these societies would be irrational not to ensure that all individuals in proportion to their capacities have access through the learning of mathematics to the careers associated with the above major works. Third, mathematics is a fund of interest to many people, both from its intrinsic nature and from the light and help it brings to other interests, whether studies or hobbies. Fourth, in a typical democracy it is most important that power should be spread; and even if much control has in the end to be concentrated in the hands of a few — politicians and experts — it is still essential that as many voices as possible should be raised, when need be, in competent criticism of the proposals and decisions of that few. But given the present stage of our civilisation, this means that as many as possible should be able to assess proposals and claims based on complex mathematical calculations; for, most of our affairs are governed in some fashion or other by mathematical considerations, or by considerations which at least require the backing of mathematical skills. Fifth, and last, it can plausibly be argued that a good number of people, perhaps most, would feel ill at ease living in a present-day developed society without having at least a minimal understanding of mathematics. For most people are conscious that mathematics has played a principal part in the progress which we count as characteristic of Western civilisation.

(6) *The natural sciences*

The reasons for the inclusion of the natural sciences in the curriculum of a typical school are much the same as those for the inclusion of mathematics. These reasons, which by now should be familiar, have been seen to come under two heads — corresponding to the two sets of aims listed earlier on — and will from now on, for the sake of convenience, be referred to under the following summary titles:

Society's collective:	*physical and material needs*
	moral needs (against violence, theft and so on)
	democratic needs (the spreading of power, equality)
	social needs (unity, co-operation)
	security needs (against external aggressions)
Individuals':	*physical and material needs*
	career possibilities and related choices
	personal development (independence and so on)
	social integration
	subjective contentedness

It should be plain without argument that in our present complex (Western liberal) societies, the natural sciences should be taught in schools, if only with an eye to ensuring that those societies *considered as wholes* have a sufficient supply of pure and applied scientists (engineers, physicists, architects and the rest) to meet their physical, material and security needs. It may be less obvious, but is not less certain, that given the state and circumstances that our societies have now reached *in fact* — that is, independently of whether or not we would like them to have taken a different path — a good number of natural scientists are also required to meet out moral, social and democratic needs. For, at least much of men's behaviour would appear to depend for its stability upon the maintenance of those material improvements brought about through the advancement and application of the natural sciences; since a fair proportion of crimes in the past arose from sheer want, and a great many more would be likely to arise in the future from any real or threatened decline in physical and material standards; and similar things may be said concerning societies' internal relations and political stability. Even if, as is sometimes objected, the results of the natural sciences have proved to be more a mixture of good and bad than was once optimistically expected, there is small doubt that over the last three and a half centuries they have contributed greatly to the improved social conditions and political balance of Western societies. Few people with a sense and knowledge of history would wish to live, for example, the life of the average city-dweller in pre-scientific eras. But in any event there is no real choice before us. Talk of a return to earlier and supposedly serener ways of life makes little sense when it suggests that we might by some supreme and unprecedented act of will abandon our science. On the contrary, the only genuine choice before us is to improve the latter; to make more careful use of it; to avoid its ills. Then, given that science is here to stay, our kinds of society will continue to require substantial numbers of scientists in order to meet their democratic needs. The reason for this is similar to that given in the discussion of mathematics: namely, that any modern democracy, if it is to retain its essential characteristics, must have a good number of people about who are able competently to question, challenge and debate the proposals and decisions of the executive few. And if one thing is now certain concerning the future it is that these proposals and decisions, like those in most other societies, will be caught up in a growingly complex web of science.

To turn now to the justification of teaching the natural sciences with a view to the needs of individuals. All children should be given the opportunity of studying the sciences for the following reasons: because this will widen their range of choice when they come to decide on a job or career; because doing so offers them the source of an absorbing interest in life; because it provides them with a grasp of much that can be of fundamental use to them (such as an understanding of the functions of the body and its health, or of electricity and mechanics); because it can enable them to feel at least moderately at home in an age and civilisation which is dominated both intellectually and practically by the sciences; because it can give them the beginnings of the sort of understanding which is required for taking part in rational discussions concerning the major moral and political issues which arise from, or involve developments in, the sciences and their dependent technologies.

(7) *Social studies*

The heading 'social studies' is meant here rather liberally to cover, and in some sense to draw together, such disciplines as sociology, history, human geography, economics, psychology and political science. However, before the place of these in the curriculum is discussed, a number of preliminary points need to be made concerning what is to be argued. First, it will be assumed that even if, for reasons of method or on some other grounds, social studies are best treated in schools as one 'subject', they are still in the end made up of those several disciplines out of which they developed and upon which, as far as can be seen, they continue to rely for their success and progress. Second, it will not be contended that each and every of these disciplines, in however integrated a manner, should have a place in the typical school curriculum; rather it will be argued that it would be irrational not to have a substantial core of them. On the other hand it will become obvious that in theory it would be perfectly rational to include them all, since for every one of them considered singly there are good grounds for its inclusion. But it is impossible to teach them all, because there is not the time, because there is rarely the competence and, more simply, because there are limits to what children can take. A core therefore is what is usually done: a core is what ought to be done.

To turn now to reasons in favour of including social studies. Their pursuit is required for the fulfilling of societies' collective needs: material, moral, democratic, defence and social. This is because if these needs are to stand a chance of being met in present-day developed societies, these latter must possess a substantial number of people with a thorough grasp of human affairs and their conditions. It is true that the social sciences have never won, and — for reasons given in Chapter 3 — cannot even aspire to the same sort of success as physics and chemistry; but it does not follow from this that any society could rationally abandon its studies of sociology, psychology and the like. For these studies at least put the facts before us in a systematic way, however poor they are in coming up with solutions. They manage to turn a vague and general awareness of a society's problems into a usefully precise description of what those problems are, how acute, where located and how widespread. For this reason every present-day society is rationally obliged to make use of the social sciences when making such decisions as those touching the organisation and financing of defence; legal procedures; prisons; police forces; pensions and psychiatric counsellors. Then again, and as usual, it is important for democracies to ensure that there are enough persons to understand and watch over these endless, costly and far-reaching decisions. It is rightly said that a healthy democracy requires public access to information; but this access to information would be of little use if no one among the public had the understanding and training required to make sense of it and, where need be, to show up its inadequacies. Finally, if social studies in schools are useful in spreading information and in producing future experts in the amassing and assessing of it, they can also be useful in furthering social tolerance and its consequent harmony. For while to understand other people's ways and beliefs is not of itself to become tolerant of them, it is a necessary condition of that democratic virtue, at least for the majority of us.

To turn now to the justification of social studies from the point of view of individuals rather than societies collectively. They provide a source of unending and absorbing interest; they open the way to careers; they can help students make sense of their lives and even choose more rationally how to live; they can help open their minds by presenting them with the ideas, successes and failures of other men; they can enable them to take an intelligent part, if they so desire, in their societies' political, social and moral debates; they can help them achieve independence of mind by measuring their beliefs against those of others. And so on.

None of these benefits follow of necessity from the teaching of social studies; but they follow from it often enough in fact to constitute its justification.

(8) *Literature*

The study of literature can be justified in many ways.

In what concerns individuals, it again opens the way to careers and is a source of interest, delight, inspiration and amusement. But there is more. It can be said to contribute in several ways to a quite special kind of development. To begin with, it brings with it an increased understanding of human actions, emotions, ideas and attitudes: an understanding of a kind very different from that contributed by the social sciences. For, while the latter are general, detached and impersonal, literature is — or can be — at once immediate, committed, vivid and concrete. It can even with some plausibility claim to be the closest form of communication with other minds that is open to us. At any rate it is the ablest expression of them. Secondly, the study of literature helps individuals to understand and direct their own ideas, emotions and attitudes. It brings into focus for them precisely which sorts of characters and characteristics they admire and which they reject; it unearths and sheds light on their own closest feelings and half-formulated opinions; it presents them with new ideas on how to live, feel, judge and act; it puts before them novel ideas, models and purposes. In short, it enables them in imagination to explore, and in reality better to choose, how they will live and what they will be. Thirdly, the study of literature helps many students to become more tolerant of the views and lives of others — though once again it has to be stressed that this consequence by no means necessarily follows, and that some literature is equally apt to produce intolerance, prejudice and hostility.

It can be added that the study of literature brings about, or can bring about, a greater command of expression and control of language, and that this in turn can make for better personal communication with others, easier participation in discussions and debates over matters of social concern, and greater confidence in the putting forward and defending of one's views.

To leave individuals aside now, we can see that societies as wholes also have good reasons for fostering the study and the production of literature. For one thing, societies take pride in what they consider to be their outstanding human achievements, and among these as a matter of sheer fact — whatever the reasons — they count their great literary works. For another thing, all societies have an interest in fostering what they know to be valued by so many of their individual members — as literature clearly is. Thirdly, societies profit from having individual members with well developed skills of communication who can carry out the tasks of being their public servants, broadcasters, educators and the like. Finally, democracies benefit from having citizens whose study of literature enables them — as editors, journalists, playwrights, novelists and so on — to take a better than average part in the open debate which as democracies they so greatly prize.

(9) *The arts*

All schools should have as part of their curriculum at least some of the arts: music, painting, drawing, sculpture, drama and the rest. The principal reasons for this are to be found already among those given as justifying literature, and need not be repeated. The following points only are worth separate mention. The first is that to judge from the sale of records, from popular radio and television programmes, music (and *mutatis mutandis* drama, dance and others of the arts) is of fundamental significance in people's lives, and on this score alone merits as high a place in the curriculum as any other pursuits. The other point is that at least certain forms of art (for example, painting and sculpture), like dress and personal appearance, are the source of strong emotional commitments and prejudices, and their inclusion in the curriculum gives schools an opportunity to get their pupils, if not to appreciate, at any rate to be tolerant of the preferences and leanings of others in these areas.

(10) *Practical skills*

The justification of the inclusion of such things as cooking, metalwork and woodwork in the curriculum again follows along familiar lines: their usefulness, interest, career prospects, and most of the other consequences that from time to time have been mentioned on behalf of this or that subject. The only point to be added is that the inclusion of a substantial amount of practical work serves the function of making clear that society genuinely values practical skills, does not consider them inferior, and does not wish to see them treated as no more than hobbies.

111

(11) *Preparation for living*

This part of the curriculum has to be left imprecise, because the problems of living, and therefore an adequate preparation to meet them, vary with time, place and most other circumstances. The problems confronting children growing up in a depressed area, for example, are different from those confronting children in a wealthy one. Because of this, when filling in the detail of the curriculum under this heading the reasonable thing to do is consult with parents, employers, pupils and the local community in general.

To take an example, however, of the sort of thing that is at issue — a great deal can be done to help pupils understand what sorts of careers or jobs are likely to be available to them, and to have some clear notion of what is involved in them. This kind of knowledge and understanding is of importance to society as a whole, since ideally it wants people to pursue its jobs and careers who are well suited to them. It is equally and obviously of importance to the interests and fulfilment of individuals. To take a related example — if there are no jobs likely to be available to some individuals in the near future, schools again must do all that they can to help; because while they may not be perfectly equipped to confront the consequent problems, no one else is likely to be of much use. Other examples of preparation for living are: sex education; the practical study of the law and of citizens' rights; a down-to-earth study of the financial entanglements that the average person is likely to get into.

To this part of the proposed curriculum, more than to most, it is sometimes objected that in including it schools are going beyond what is their proper concern. Their task, it is said, is to 'educate', not to play the role of social worker, counsellor and priest. But this objection is groundless. The job of the schools is to carry out what society in general requires them to carry out; and while society does of course require that schools 'educate' their pupils (interpreting 'educate' here as to do with academic matters), it also requires that they contribute what commonsense dictates is needed for the well-being both of society as a whole and of its individual members. Experience reveals that if sex education, preparation for careers and the rest, are not undertaken at school, they are rarely undertaken at all. And it can be pointed out anyway that preparation for life does not have to loom excessively large in the curriculum: for the most part it can be carried out alongside other studies and activities.

Compulsory and optional elements in the curriculum

The components of the curriculum so far discussed are to be considered compulsory. That is, in ordinary circumstances, all schools, to leave aside the distinction between primary and secondary, must teach them, and to all pupils at some stage of their careers. (With respect to social studies, the arts and practical skills, a representative selection is to be taught, not of course every possible candidate in the running.) The justification of this compulsoriness is that the subjects concerned are so closely tied to the aims of societies for themselves and their individual members, that it would be irrational of any society to leave them open to choice.

If this sounds unduly harsh, it should be borne in mind that compulsion does not mean brutality; nor does it mean affronting personal liberties. Parents compel their children to do and not to do all manner of things without being brutal to them or affronting them, and societies use compulsion in such matters as taxation or traffic laws again without brutality or affront. Further, every allowance may be made for exceptional cases. For example, if teachers judge that for one reason or another a given individual or group of individuals should not be made to do this or that subject, this is perfectly acceptable and rational; provided it is understood that the onus is on the teachers in question to provide adequate reasons for their judgment. Again, that subjects are compulsory has no bearing, or should have no bearing, on the manner in which they are to be presented; if anything, the very fact that they are compulsory should urge teachers to make them as lively and interesting as they can. Finally, a principal purpose behind making compulsory the components of the curriculum so far discussed is precisely to extend children's *liberty of choice* in their future careers, ways of life and interests. A child who is left free not to read and write, or to learn nothing of science and society, is thereby excluded from most careers and from most interests as well.

To turn now to *optional* subjects. These are of the kind which it is perfectly rational for a society to allow or even positively to encourage, but which it does not have to insist on; they are not *essential* to the furthering of its aims. Examples of these are: chess, crime-detection, fire-fighting, hairdressing, car driving, parachuting, sailing and wallpapering.

Inevitably there are points of difficulty attaching to this area of the curriculum, since there is not always agreement over what is essential, nor even over what it is proper for schools to undertake. It will not be possible to look at and form an opinion on all of the cases which have given rise to discussion and disagreement, but two examples may serve at least to illustrate the kinds of issues involved, and to suggest possible ways of meeting them. Many teachers for a long time have argued that foreign languages should be made or kept compulsory in the curriculum on the grounds that they are important for more than one reason: for trade; for overcoming ingrained habits of insularity and xenophobia; for improving international understanding and relations; for providing careers and interests. Others have argued to the contrary. They have reasoned that most of the benefits mentioned above can be attained easily enough through literature in translation or through social studies; and that needs for the languages themselves can be satisfied through tertiary and other courses. They add that the great amount of time and effort required to master a language at school (a rare achievement, they claim) is altogether out of proportion to the benefits to be derived from it. In cases of this kind, where arguments on both sides are genuinely persuasive, the best solution might be to distinguish what should be compulsory for a typical school as a whole from what should be compulsory for a typical student. Languages may well be important enough to warrant their compulsory inclusion in the curriculum, but not important enough (or too difficult, or whatever) to warrant making all students attempt them.

The second example of an optional subject which on and off has given rise to argument and disagreement is 'religion'. However, the disagreement here has usually been due to a failure to distinguish between 'religion' as a study *about* people's religious beliefs and customs (an area of enquiry belonging properly to the social sciences) and 'religion' as a course designed to awaken religious feelings and to elicit or preserve religious commitment. Those arguing in favour of 'religion' have usually had in mind the study of religious beliefs and practices as an important means to the understanding of their own and others' cultures. Those arguing against it have usually had in mind organised attempts to get children to *be* religious. Once this argument at cross purposes has been cleared up, the solution to the problem is plain. In Western liberal democracies there is as much to be said in favour of 'religion' as part of social studies as in favour of any other component of that subject. By contrast, there is no case for imposing a course designed to make pupils 'believers'. If courses of the latter kind are ever offered at all, they should be matters of choice both to individual pupils and to the schools themselves.

A final point of difficulty is that often the subjects or courses suggested for classification as optional are seen by some as so closely analogous to related compulsory subjects that they wish them to be accorded the same standing. Some, for example, wish to argue that wallpapering, car-maintenance or fire-fighting should be allowed to count as practical subjects alongside metalwork and carpentry. There can be no hard and fast rule for settling issues of this kind, but the following procedure seems justifiable. If a course may fairly be held to deal with basic principles having a wide variety of applications, it should be allowed to count as an element in a compulsory subject. If on the other hand it is narrowly circumscribed and does not teach principles having wide applications beyond itself, it should not. Metalwork is an example of the former; wallpapering of the latter.

Some objections

The autonomy of teachers

Now that the theory of the curriculum in terms of rationality has been set out and a typical content derived from it, it will be useful to look at the principal objections likely to be raised against it.

The first of these is that in appealing as it does to the desires and wishes of society, it constitutes a denial of the professional rights and autonomy of teachers. This objection however may be met by the following comments. First, teachers undeniably possess a considerable amount of expertise, and this forms a basis for according them both rights and a measure of autonomy. For example, as a body they have given more systematic thought than most to what children should learn at school, and individually they are at least moderately accomplished in some area or areas of study and activity. Again, whether corporately or individually, they have a fair knowledge of child psychology and other disciplines related to education, and they have acquired an unrivalled body of experience concerning what specific choices in curriculum-content and what methods employed in the teaching of them are likely to be successful. For reasons of this kind it would plainly be irrational of a society not to pay heed to them, and not to support a degree of autonomy befitting their skills, experience and learning — in a word their expertise. However, this expertise does not extend to the settling of what the underlying aims of a curriculum should be; and, as was argued earlier, no other expertise either can properly claim to extend so far. Neither teachers nor any professional body can, for example, tell us as a result of expertise that all individuals should be educated to choose which way of life to lead, or within the limits of their ability what career to pursue: and insofar as aims of this kind dictate the content of a curriculum, as according to the argument of this chapter they do, teachers have no expertise in respect of the latter either. All societies then, particularly democratic societies, would be foolish to allow them to behave as if they did.

Secondly, teachers are not reduced to some sort of servility when and because a minimum curriculum is imposed upon them. As members of a democracy they have a right to take part in society's deliberations concerning the content of the curriculum, and both their professional integrity and individual use of reason require of them that they offer their advice and express their opinions concerning it, since they more than most have thought about it. But equally their integrity and reason demand that they stay within the boundaries of their professional competence.

Thirdly, it should be borne in mind that a minimum curriculum is imposed upon teachers in countries of very diverse political kinds — as in Russia, France and Sweden — without this being widely considered an affront to the professional competence of the teachers in question. Even in England, where the curriculum is in theory left to governing bodies or the like, society exerts such pressures that the freedom of these bodies is tightly circumscribed: they cannot, for example, easily go about dropping such subjects as mathematics or reading, since the reactions to such moves when they are attempted are considerable, however slow in gathering force.

A second objection to the theory of this chapter is that it does nothing but preserve the *status quo*, and that this can be seen at once from the content supposedly derivable from it.

This objection is not very convincing. Apart from the fact that the *status quo* it refers to is of but short historical standing, no society has to preserve this or any other *status quo*. The rational application and balancing up of a society's aims is likely to shift with changes in circumstances, and when these occur the contents of its curriculum will have to shift too. On the other hand there plainly are limits to the sorts of shifts that might seriously be contemplated. It is not likely, for instance, that in the predictable future children in our societies will not need to read, write and talk with fluency. Nor is it likely that our societies will cease to expect their schools to contribute to the health and well-being of their pupils, or to take part in the background preparation of doctors, lawyers, industrial experts and the rest.

It is worth commenting further that in the light of what has previously been argued in this and earlier chapters, if individual teachers or groups of teachers dislike or even despise the present *status quo*, they have no right to attempt to alter it by bypassing the procedures of democracy. For by their having 'no right' is meant here, as follows from previous analyses, that society would be irrational to tolerate their doing anything of the kind. And that would seem to be obvious.

If this sounds threatening, it should be recalled that in present-day Western liberal societies a considerable degree of initiative and freedom to experiment is conceded anyway under the rubric of acceptable democratic procedures. Further, it has already been allowed that considerable freedom should be left to teachers (and other experts) in judging such things as how much a given subject should be taught; when it should be taught and by what methods; which students should be exempt from it. On the other hand this was not meant to imply that teachers should do as they please in these matters. It was stressed that the onus of giving adequate reasons is on the teachers themselves and the experts they consult, when they decide that such and such a child or group of children should not study mathematics, or in some other way should cease to be in the running for a wide choice of careers and ways of living.

The fundamental rights of parents

The present theory, it might be objected, threatens to undermine the basic rights of parents. But this is not so. Instead of undermining them it explains and supports them. It does this precisely by appealing to the fact that for a number of reasons it would be irrational of society not to take serious account of parents' goals and aversions in what concerns the upbringing of their children. For example, parents are the single biggest influence on their children. Parents typically have a greater interest in and commitment to the future of their children than anyone else has. Again, the co-operation of parents in the processes of education is usually more important than any other factor, since the part they play particularly early on is not easily dispensed with. Finally, if the curriculum of schools did run seriously counter to the basic wishes of parents for their children, there would soon be wide-spread dissatisfaction in society: for parents constitute a sizeable and important section of it.

In short, the present theory of the curriculum makes sense of and supports parents' rights. At the same time, being essentially a moderate theory it acknowledges the rights of children, teachers, administrators and other groups in society.

Knowledge as worthwhile in itself and as an ideal

The last objection that will be looked at is that the theory of this chapter seriously undervalues knowledge and learning. Education, it is urged, should be seen as an end in itself and one of the highest ideals of the West; to treat it as something less is to demean if not to destroy it.

Philosophers in recent years have shown little enthusiasm for talk of ideals or of things worthwhile in themselves, and sometimes even refuse to allow sense to these notions altogether. But in this they are wrong: there is nothing odd or unintelligible about either notion. To say that something (happiness, for example) is worthwhile in itself is not to say that it is possessed of some strange sort of property, intuited by the mind alone. It is to say rather that the thing in question does not need to be pursued for the sake of something else: that it can stand on its own. For example, cleaning the house will be accepted by most people as needing to be pursued for the sake of something beyond it (health perhaps or pleasing appearances). By contrast, happiness will be considered to be worth pursuing *not* for the sake of something beyond it: it will be held to be worthwhile in itself.

Second, to say that something is pursued as an *ideal* is to say at least the following. It is pursued as something worthwhile in itself. It is held to be of unusually high worth; though not necessarily higher than all other things. While considered to be unattainable in full, it is nonetheless thought worth pursuing with as much energy and tenacity of purpose as can be mustered. In this sence, chivalry was an ideal of the fourteenth century: social justice and equality are ideals of the twentieth. There is nothing difficult in grasping the sense of all this. The notion of a thing's being worthwhile in itself has already been dealt with. The idea of a thing's having a high value relative to others is not obscure; since all of us are compelled from time to time to grade the things we prize. Finally, the notion of something's being not fully attainable but nonetheless worth striving for is again familiar to most of us: we try for the perfect late-cut in cricket or for the perfect essay in philosophy.

With these points in mind we can now turn to the question of the worth of knowledge. To begin with, it seems impossible to think of knowledge as worthwhile in itself: *separately* from the interest to be found in it. Knowledge which interests no one can hardly be thought of as worthwhile in itself; and knowledge which positively bores everyone is beyond a doubt not worthwhile in itself. At the same time it is equally impossible to think of the interest men find in knowledge as separate from that knowledge itself, as though the selfsame interest might have been caused by something other than knowledge. Indeed it is absurd to suggest, for example, that the interest I am deriving from the cognitive elements of this present argument might have been produced by something else (a drug perhaps) without my having philosophical reflections at all.

From these considerations it would seem to be more correct to speak of *interest-in-knowledge* — or, less artificially, of *interesting knowledge* — as being what is worthwhile in itself; rather than knowledge *tout court*. Physics, history and philosophy, for example, are worthwhile in themselves because they are examples of *interesting knowledge*, not just any knowledge.

If this way of understanding the claim that knowledge is worthwhile in itself is accepted, the objection raised at the beginning of this section will be seen to be without force. For the theory of the curriculum in this chapter attaches *very* great importance to men's interests in life, and it is therefore in no way incompatible with the claim that knowledge is worthwhile in itself or that it is worth pursuing as an ideal. It is not even incompatible with the claim, though it does not make it, that (interesting) knowledge is more worthwhile than the rest of the aims which Western democracies pursue on behalf of their members. What it *is* incompatible with is the claim that knowledge is worthwhile in an absolute sense — that is, even independently of men's finding an interest in it — and that this absolute worth is what justifies the pursuit of knowledge in schools. But in spite of what is often said, perhaps no one ever intended to advance that doctrine anyway.

Other theories

Children's interests and needs[2]

It will be useful now, however briefly, to compare the theory of the curriculum defended in this chapter with some of its principal rivals, and to point out the weaknesses of the latter.

The first of these is that the curriculum should centre on and be determined by the nature, needs and interests of children: find out what the latter need and you find out what should go on in schools.

If we assume that concepts like 'need' and 'interest' are sufficiently precise to be of use at all, there are still several weaknesses to this attempt to start from the point of view of the child. The first is that it assumes, or at least provokes the strong temptation to assume, that all the needs of children exist *naturally*: that is, independently of the societies into which they are born. But unless the sense of the word 'needs' is tailored *ad hoc*, this assumption is false. Children do have certain given needs – to eat, sleep, communicate, be loved, be happy and so on – but they have others which depend on their circumstances and their societies. A child born and living in London, for example, will need to learn English, to learn something of English mores and to survive in an industrial society. Needs of this sort are not given by nature, at any rate not as they stand: no one can naturally be a twentieth-century Englishman.

More fundamentally, this child-centred theory, unless very carefully qualified, is too narrow. No one should doubt that teachers ought to pay attention to their pupils' (present *and* future) needs and interests, just as they ought to pay attention to their pupils' capacities, abilities and levels of attainment. Further, it may readily be admitted that schools have not always paid sufficient heed to their pupils' point of view. Children matter, and any theory which tends to undervalue their importance is unacceptable. But equally unacceptable is a theory which undervalues the rest of society. Children constitute only one part of society, and not in all respects the most important part of it; it would therefore be irrational to devise or countenance a curriculum treating them as if they constituted the whole of it. Schools exist for children, but not for children alone.

Schools as reformers of society[3]

A theory quite opposed to the one just discussed is that schools and their curricula should be thought of not as institutions meeting their pupils' needs, but as a main and radical means of changing society. If there are inequalities, it says, or class struggles, problems of overpopulation and the like, it is the task of schools to set about countering these ills, and by shaping the attitudes of their pupils to alter the rest of society.

Educators who advance this theory have an unreal idea of their influence on society, but what they hold is untenable on other grounds anyway. Their theory allows an unreasonable and disproportionate responsibility to be placed on children for the reforming of society, and is in effect as extreme in its society-centredness as the last theory was in its child-centredness. Secondly, it is a theory which, as it is in fact applied, deprives children of much of their liberty of choice. For its adherents often argue that much of the curriculum in present-day schools is the expression of middle-class or some other bias, and as a consequence teach less of such subjects as mathematics and science than otherwise they might. But this means that their pupils are not in a position later on to make up *their own minds* about what they will do with their lives. The advantages then lie with those whose parents are able to supply what the teachers will not. One might add that while it may or may not be a good thing for a child to remain outside of the middle or any other class, it is not a good thing when this results from the ideological decision of teachers.

It will perhaps be objected here that democracies, being of their nature tolerant societies, should allow for every kind of school curriculum. But clearly they should not. Democracies should not allow schools or any other institutions seriously to interfere with what they hold to be the important interests of their members: of such interfering institutions they should be implacably intolerant.

Acquaintance with forms of knowledge[4]

A widespread theory in recent years has been that education's principal concern is with the handing on of knowledge and the developing of children's rationality. In addition, and this perhaps is the most original part of the theory, it has been claimed that knowledge can be split down into a number of distinct *a priori* forms, and that the curriculum should consist chiefly in an initiation into these forms (mathematics, physical sciences, history, and the rest).

There are several drawbacks to this theory. From the outset there has been no agreement about what the supposed principal forms of knowledge are, and it is doubtful anyway that there is a uniquely specifiable number of them. Further, even if it turned out that there were such things as forms of knowledge, it would not follow straight off that all of them should become part of a typical curriculum. Let us suppose that formal logic turned out to be one. It would not at once be evident that formal logic should become part of the curriculum. Or let us suppose that there turned out to be fifty or more distinct forms of knowledge. What would we do then?

In any event this theory of the curriculum is unnecessarily and unjustifiably narrow. Knowledge — or, to recall what was said earlier, *interesting* knowledge — and the development of rationality are not the sole aims behind the curriculum, and *a fortiori* should not uniquely determine it. Happiness, self-confidence, tolerance, liberty of choice, and many other things besides are equally important.

Utilitarian theories[5]

A number of attempts have been made to derive a typical curriculum from the tenets of utilitarianism: particularly from the basic claim that what in the end matters and matters alone is that people should gain pleasure and happiness, and correspondingly be free from misery, anxiety and other ills.

If the notions of pleasure, happiness and their opposites are so liberalised that they become co-extensive with everything that societies and individuals have as their aims, the theory of the curriculum defended in this chapter may be counted utilitarian. But to liberalise the notions in this way is to take away the attractive point of utilitarianism: namely, the providing of a single easy test for telling us *which* of our aims should be pursued and which should not. If on the other hand these notions are employed in their usual sense, the attempt to make pleasure and happiness the yardstick of what individuals and societies should aim at in life or in a curriculum is too confining. For individuals and societies have a plurality of aims, neither reducible to pleasure and happiness nor necessarily accompanied by them. For example, I may aim at being successful in business, or in achieving power, or simply in keeping my promises. None of these goals is reducible to pleasure and happiness, nor necessarily results in them. Indeed it is possible to insist that pleasure and happiness are at stake here only by altering the meanings of words, or by claiming that unconsciously (and mistakenly) I seek to derive pleasure and happiness from my pursuits. The latter is an implausible move. The former is an empty one.

The more reasonable view then to take is the one adhered to in this and earlier chapters: that men both singly and collectively have a diversity of aims, only one of which is the pursuit of pleasure and happiness. It is these many aims which should govern the curriculum.

Cultural relativism and the curriculum

Cognitive content

The last question to be looked at in this chapter is whether or not, or perhaps to what extent, the curriculum is a matter of cultural relativity. In fact there are two quite distinct questions here, the first concerning the content of the curriculum (in particular its cognitive content) and the second concerning its choice.

As was pointed out in the Introduction, the severest of the attacks made on the objectivity of the curriculum in recent years has aimed at its cognitive content: claiming that since all knowledge is relative and culturally determined, what usually passes for objective knowledge is what this or that power-group in society wishes to pass as such. The principal aim of this book, and the exclusive aim of its first five chapters, has been precisely to counter this attack and to show that the chief areas in which men commonly claim to have knowledge and objective learning — 'commonsense', the natural sciences, the social sciences and morality — are not areas of cultural relativity at all.

If the arguments developed were successful, it follows that *none* of the cognitive (opposed to skill-constituted) elements of the curriculum are culturally relative. It follows that moral education, the natural sciences, social studies, and all developments of commonsense are not, because that was *explicitly* argued for. It follows that the cognitive components of health education, literature and preparation for living are not, since these are dependent upon one or more of the former. It follows for the same reason that none of those cognitive elements in the curriculum are relative which are incidental to or associated with the study of the arts, basic skills, practical skills and character education. That leaves mathematics, and while the status of claims in the latter is beyond the scope of this book, this much at least can be said. The basic elements of mathematics — the concepts of number, addition, subtraction and the rest — are as much part of our 'commonsense' as are the elements of logic or the grasp of such things as causality or the concept of material objects. So they are not matters of cultural relativity. This is indicated by the simple fact that all men know that $2 + 2 = 4$, and that it is unintelligible to suggest that some cultures, having understood the meaning of such statements, might choose to deny or dispense with them. Secondly, the claims made within applied mathematics may for the most part be taken as empirical claims anyway, and therefore as no more culturally relative than any others of the kind.

Choice of content

It is often said that whether or not knowledge is objective, there are wide differences in curriculum-content from culture to culture, and moreover that this is as it should be: that there is not and could not be one curriculum suitable for all cultures and societies.

These remarks are just, and should serve as corrective reminders to us if and when we are tempted to impose programmes of learning upon those to whom they are both unacceptable and ill-adapted. However, they should not be confused with the remarks of the radical relativist. The latter holds not only that there are and should be curriculum differences from culture to culture, but that there are no rational constraints setting limits on these differences. He holds, that is, that there are no common elements imposed by human reason upon the curriculum, wherever it is to be found, and that accordingly it makes no sense to speak of what all rational men are bound to choose when placed in like circumstances. What men are bound to choose, he says, is determined by their respective cultures, not by principles supposedly common to all men.

The radical relativist is wrong on several heads, and the first point that may be brought against him is this. Those who share his doctrine often attempt to argue for fundamental curriculum changes. But to do this is to assume beforehand that there are common rational principles and premises (common at least to themselves and to those whom they address) which enable men to compare curricula and to judge that some are right to the exclusion of others.

Second, it is worth pointing out that the whole venture of having a curriculum at all, to use that word now in a rather more liberalised sense, is not a matter of choice for this or that culture, but is a matter of human nature. For human beings, particularly when young, need to be *taught* if they are successfully to co-operate as members of society.

Third, it was argued earlier in this chapter that there are aims common to all groups of men, and correspondingly a set of principles dictating in however broad an outline what every curriculum must contain. For example, it was argued that every curriculum must contain elements for ensuring health, moral behaviour, material well-being and social cohesion. There is no room for cultural choice here.

This point is a conclusive refutation of the extreme relativist claim that curriculum-content is on all fronts a matter of cultural choice. However, it may now be objected that as soon as we get away from high-level description and principle, what is taught in this or that society is after all a matter of relativity. Western liberal democracies teach physics, chemistry, symphonic structure and the history of Renaissance art; other societies teach none of these. Both sorts of society are right.

It may well be that both of these sorts of society are right. But it they are, this does not have to be because their choices are governed by culturally relative preferences and principles. It may be because they are governed by what would govern all rational men in like circumstances. Moreover, with respect to the major cognitive components of the curriculum, this is precisely what obtains. To illustrate this point with an example, all human beings have an aversion to disease and to seeing their children die young. But evils of this kind are largely checked where there is a reasonable level of engineering skill and medical competence. If follows that any society which is in the position to acquire the requisite level of engineering and medicine ought to do so, and ought to ensure that what is acquired is passed on through education. Thus those societies which in fact possess and educate in these skills do so not because they have made a culturally relative choice, but because they have made a choice which is humanly rational. Societies which do not possess them are exempt from blame only because they have not been able to (because of grinding poverty, ignorance or the like).

Some will perhaps be hostile to this line of reasoning, on the grounds that such things as engineering and medicine have brought men more harm than good. But this hostility, however well founded, has no relevance to the problem of cultural relativism. On the contrary, if it could be established that engineering and medicine do greater harm than good to men, and that these evils are not capable of being countered, there would be no question of relative choice open to any of us. We would be compelled by reason to abandon the skills at issue as fast as we could.

FURTHER READING

Some of the books included here are general introductions to the Philosophy of Education.

Archambault, R.D. (ed.) *Philosophical Analysis and Education*, London, 1965.
Bantock, G.H. *Culture, Industrialisation and Education*, London, 1968.
*Barrow, R. *Common Sense and the Curriculum*, London, 1976.
*Barrow, R. *Radical Education*, London, 1978.
*Bernbaum, G. *Knowledge and Ideology in the Sociology of Education*, London, 1977.
Bruner, J.S. *The Relevance of Education*, London, 1972.
Cooper, D.E. *Illusions of Equality*, London, 1980.
*Dearden, R.F. *The Philosophy of Primary Education*, London, 1968.
Dearden, R.F. *Problems in Primary Education*, London, 1976.
Dearden, R.F., Hirst, P.H. and Peters, R.S. *Education and the Development of Reason*, London, 1972.
Dewey, J. *Experience and Education*, New York, 1938.
Eliot, T.S. *Notes Towards a Definition of Culture*, London, 1948.
Flew, A. *Sociology, Equality and Education*, London, 1976.
*Freire, P. *Pedagogy of the Oppressed*, London, 1972.
*Hamilton, D. *Curriculum Evaluation*, London, 1976.
Hardie, C.D. *Truth and Fallacy in Education*, London, 1942.
Hirst, P. *Knowledge and the Curriculum*, London, 1975.
Hirst, P.H. "The Curriculum and its Objectives", *Studies in Education 2. The Curriculum*, London, 1975.
Hirst, P.H. and Peters, R.S. *The Logic of Education*, London, 1970.
Hollins, T.H.B. (ed.) *Aims in Education: The Philosophic Approach*, Manchester, 1964.
Hooper, R. (ed.) *The Curriculum: Context, Design and Development*, Edinburgh, 1971.
*Hopkins, A. *The School Debate*, London, 1978.
*Illich, I.D. *Deschooling Society*, London, 1971.
*Jenkins, D. and Shipman, M.D. *Curriculum: an Introduction*, London, 1976.
*Keddie, N. (ed.) *Tinker, Tailor: The Myth of Cultural Deprivation*, London, 1973.
*Kelly, A.V. *The Curriculum. Theory and Practice*, London, 1977.
*Langford, G. *Philosophy and Education*, London, 1968.
Lawton, D. *Social Change, Educational Theory and Curriculum Planning*, London, 1973.
*Lawton, D. *Class, Culture and the Curriculum*, London, 1975.
Lloyd, D.I. (ed.) *Philosophy and the Teacher*, London, 1976.
MacDonald, B. and Walker, R. *Changing the Curriculum*, London, 1976.
Nisbet, P. *Purpose in the Curriculum*, London, 1957.
O'Connor, D.J. *An Introduction to the Philosophy of Education*, London, 1957.
Peters, R.S. *Ethics and Education*, London, 1965.
Peters, R.S. *The Concept of Education*, London, 1967.
Peters, R.S. (ed.) *The Philosophy of Education*, Oxford, 1973.
Phenix, P.H. *Realms of Meaning*, New York, 1964.
*Pring, R. *Knowledge and Schooling*, London, 1976.
Reid, L.A. *Philosophy and Education*, London, 1962.
Reynolds, J. and Skilbeck, M. *Culture and the Classroom*, London, 1976.
*Sarup, M. *Marxism and Education*, London, 1978.

Scheffler, I. *The Language of Education,* Springfield, 1960.
Scheffler, I. *Conditions of Knowledge,* Glenview, 1965.
Sockett, H. *Designing the Curriculum,* London, 1976.
*Tibble, J.W. *The Study of Education,* London, 1966.
Warnock, M. *Schools of Thought,* London, 1977.
*White, J.P. *Towards a Compulsory Curriculum,* London, 1973.
Whitehead, A.N. *The Aims of Education,* London, 1932.
Wilson, P.S. *Interest and Discipline in Education,* London, 1971.
Woods, R.G. and Barrow, R. *Introduction to the Philosophy of Education,* London, 1975.
Young, M. (ed.) *Knowledge and Control,* London, 1971.

CHAPTER 7
TRANSCULTURAL RELATIVISM

It was mentioned in the Introduction that in the recent debate over knowledge and teaching, the following sorts of claims have been made by writers such as Young, Esland, Bourdieu, Blum and Gorbutt: that knowledge is not something out there, independent of people knowing; that man makes his own world; that knowledge at all levels is relativised and the possibility of absolute knowledge is denied; that knowledge is one perspective through which one sees the world. The same writers hold further that knowledge is a social product, constantly 'legitimated' by those in positions of power and control; that there are alternative ways of seeing reality and organising experience; that these different ways are equally valid; that there is always the possibility of change in how we see things and consequently in our assertions about what are to count as matters of truth, reality and knowledge. Finally they go on to draw some radical conclusions concerning schools. The curriculum, they say, is in every society derived from its culture; that what passes as knowledge in the curriculum is what teachers and others in power wish to be passed as such; that the way in which pupils see things is different from the way in which the teachers themselves see them, and that it cannot be said *a priori* that the latter are right.

So far in this book it has been argued to the contrary that knowledge is not what those in power wish to count as such; that what is true is not relative to this or that culture or cultures; that the cognitive content of a justifiable curriculum is not in any non-trivial sense determined by the culture of a society or societies. In brief, the first six chapters of this book have argued against the cultural-relativist conclusions of Young and his colleagues, and they have done this by trying to show systematically what could *not* justifiably be meant by the statements of these and other writers.

The following important question needs yet to be faced. Is there nothing at all behind the assertions of Young and others that knowledge is not something 'out there', that it can never be absolute? It would be surprising if this were so, since from the time of Protagoras the doctrine of relativism has persisted in one form or another, and even Plato himself espoused it as true of the perceptible world. But it is not so, and this chapter will accordingly argue that while the doctrine of cultural relativism is altogether untenable — for the reasons given over the last six chapters — the doctrine of transcultural relativism has very strong arguments in its favour. This means that Young and his colleagues may after all be right in holding that knowledge is not absolute, and correct in their attacks on the traditional doctrines of empiricism and rationalism. If they are, then they are wrong not in the most fundamental part of their thesis but in the conclusions which they wish to draw from it, and in the related explanations they attempt of knowledge and reality in terms of cultures and power-groups.

The nature of transcultural relativism

Cultural relativism is the doctrine that the truth of men's beliefs is relative to and determined by this or that sub-group to which severally they belong: to nation, class, religion, civilisation or whatever. By contrast, transcultural relativism is the doctrine that the nature of men's apprehension, grasp or awareness of reality is not relative to this or that particular sub-group or culture, but to mankind as a whole, or perhaps to all intelligent, sentient creatures.

This doctrine of transcultural relativism may further be characterised in two complementary ways. The first of these is to say that the manner in which men apprehend reality does not reveal how the latter stands absolutely: that is, how it stands independently of its being apprehended. This assertion can be made intuitively clearer by a comparison with the lower-level claim that men's *visual* apprehension of reality does not reveal how the latter is: that while initially we see the world as if in itself coloured, reason and reflection force us to the view that it is not. By analogy, the manner in which we apprehend reality *conceptually* may lead us at first to think that we are able to describe it as it is independently of us. But, the transcultural relativist argues, reason will force us again to think otherwise.

The second way of characterising transcultural relativism may be put as follows. There are good reasons (to be gone into later) for holding that men's apprehension or awareness of reality is not direct or immediate, but that it takes place through 'representations'. There are good reasons too for holding that there are, or could be, alternative sets of representations through which intelligent beings do, or might, apprehend reality. On the assumption that these claims are intelligible, transcultural relativism may be defined as the doctrine that while there are, or may be, alternative sets of representations and corresponding beliefs through which intelligent beings apprehend reality, it makes no sense to say that one of these sets is, or may be, correct to the exclusion of others.

Evolution

The case supporting transcultural relativism may now be outlined as follows.

If men wish seriously to reflect on the nature of reality, there is no choice before them but to start from where they are, to start from whatever is the best account of things available to them at their own particular period of time. In what concerns us — in the twentieth-century — the best account of things before us is the one which contains *inter alia* the well established theories of science, and among these in turn the theory of evolution.

According to this last theory, the properties which we count as characteristic of the human organism, like those of others, are properties which initially arose as mutations from earlier forms, and which have for the most part proved useful to man's survival. In other words, the function of the properties of the human organism, including those of the organs of sense, the brain and the rest of the cognitive system, is to be seen as one of adaptation and survival, not as one of discovering how reality is when divorced from our apprehending it. We have neither *a priori* nor empirical grounds for assuming that what is needed for our adapting and consequently surviving is that our representations should reveal reality as it is *in se*.

This consideration by itself is negative. It allows us at most to conclude that we lack sufficient grounds for seeing ourselves as able to discover reality as it is in itself. A further consideration, however, gives us positive grounds for saying that we are not thus able. This consideration is as follows. If we examine the evolutionary scale, we find that there is in point of structure and complexity an almost indefinite range of organisms: starting with the protozoa or thereabouts, and reaching as far as (or beyond) such organisms as our own. There is at the same time a corresponding diversity of adaptations to environment, and where these latter take the form of apprehension or awareness, they too are found to be almost endless in variety. But once we grant all this, what grounds can we discover, apart from self-indulgence, for asserting that human apprehension is more disposed than others to reveal the nature of reality as it is in itself? If we see things with proper modesty and look upon our forms of awareness (perceiving, conceptualising and so on) as the properties of one kind of organism among the numberless many, all of which adapt more or less successfully to their environment — if we see all this, we must surely judge it unreasonable to single ourselves out from the many, asserting that unlike others we are able to grasp reality as it is in itself. We have more reason to believe that we are not.

The incompatibility of objects of awareness

There is the following *prima facie* objection to the above argument. It does nothing to show that different organisms may not severally but correctly apprehend partial aspects of the selfsame reality as it is in itself. However, this objection may be met by two further arguments which give support to transcultural relativism. The first of these is as follows. No two things incompatible with each other can simultaneously be identical with a third; if they were, the latter would be rendered self-contradictory. Because of this, the ways in which reality appears to us cannot be taken to be identical with reality as it is in itself, since the latter appears to us in forms which are not only different but incompatible. For example, the form in which it presents itself to our bare senses is different from and incompatible with the manner in which it presents itself through optical and electron-microscopes, or through such other devices as are adapted to our non-visual means of perception. To the bare retina (and to other sense-receptors *mutatis mutandis*) the world appears as containing material objects: bodies of gross and bulky proportions. But these objects do not appear when light is differently refracted, through the lenses of microscopes. Does reality as it is in itself then, or does it not, contain such objects? The initial temptation is to answer that it does and that it contains whatever else is perceived microscopically or otherwise. But this temptation should be resisted for at least two reasons. First, reality as it is in itself cannot be said at the same time to contain both gross bodies as they appear to our unaided retinae *and* such things as molecules or electrons, which are detected only indirectly. For these sorts of item are endowed with incompatible properties. Gross bodies as they appear to our unaided vision (and to our other senses, again *mutatis mutandis*) have continuous surfaces; as they appear through optical microscopes, they have surfaces which are highly discontinuous; as they appear through electron-microscopes, it is hard to think of them as having surfaces at all. We might try to meet the dilemma which results from this by taking one of two directions. We might choose to say that gross bodies are the ultimate components of reality and that molecules, electrons and so on are but constructs and appearances. Or we might prefer the assertion that electrons, molecules and the rest are reality's ultimate parts, with gross bodies as but their appearances. But neither of these moves is satisfactory. For, on the one hand, the assertions and theories of science are both too coherent and too explanatory for us to dismiss the micro-entities they refer to as mere constructs or appearances. Those entities, or at any rate something closely resembling them, have at present *as good an entitlement* to be taken as real as do tables and chairs when these are not perceived. On the other hand, there are no convincing arguments to support the belief that what contemporary science has to say concerning the ultimate constituents of reality is either final or approaching final. As likely as not the progress of science on this point will be unending, and this urges the conclusion that we can never answer questions such as: What is reality like in itself? We can only answer questions of the following kind: What are our present and most reasonable representations of reality like?

To this it might be objected that it is still *in principle* possible to attain a set of representations capable of disclosing the nature of reality in itself. But this objection may be met by the third argument to support transcultural relativism.

The indirect nature of our representations

A summary of this third argument will best begin with a series of points in favour of the case for the *indirectness* of man's grasp of reality. These are as follows:

(i)   On the most rational account of things acceptable to us at present, whenever we perceive something, information passes from that thing to our brain and this information even changes form in the course of its passage: it changes, for example, from light- or sound-waves, or from pressure at the body's extremities, to electrical impulses moving along the afferent nerves to the cerebral cortex. Because of this we receive information from the world, not the world itself; we apprehend encoded information, not the source of that information.

(ii)   In every case of sense-perception, a time-interval must elapse between the initiating activity of the object which is to be perceived and our perceiving it. The visual experience of distant stars is a striking example of this, but it is only an example – no different in kind from our hearing, tasting, feeling or whatever. It follows that any object which is perceived could in theory cease to exist before the perceiver is made aware of it. It follows too, and in turn, that unless we allow direct perception of the past, objects of perception can only mediately be perceived.

(iii)   Hallucination-states, dream-states, and even illusion-states are sometimes indistinguishable in point of their immediately perceived properties from non-hallucinatory, non-illusory and waking states. A simple, if not the simplest, way to account for this indistinguishability is to say that, waking or sleeping (and so on for the rest), we are not directly confronted with reality; that the latter is given to us through interpreted representations.

(iv)   We have good grounds to believe that even our most down-to-earth observations are theory-laden; that what we perceive is the result of expectations, hopes, beliefs, inferences and so on. Stated more generally, what we perceive depends on the structure and present state of our mind or brain. It is because of this that in spite of continued efforts neither philosophers nor psychologists have been able to lay bare an ultimate given. But if there is no settled, no ultimate given, what directly we apprehend must be no more than a series of highly patterned representations; not reality in itself confronting us face to face.

Considerations of this kind lead us to conclude that the objects of our immediate apprehension or acquaintance are but 'inner' representations. But of course we have at the same time every reason to believe that there is a reality external to us, responsible for both the being and nature of those representations. For the objects of our awareness are for the most part not subject to our volition, either in existence, timing or content. So, to dismiss the existence of an independent reality would be not only to embrace solipsism, but to believe in a series of coincidences (among our representations) altogether too vast to be seriously credible.

However, once we acknowledge the existence of an independent reality responsible for and standing in some kind of causal relationship to our representations, we are led to ask if these representations *resemble* reality, thus indirectly revealing its nature and intrinsic properties. To this question there are no *a priori* grounds for answering Yes, and what empirical evidence we have leads us to answer No. This empirical evidence, very briefly, is that whenever we significantly alter the state of our organs of perception and apprehension, we alter at the same time the way in which the world presents itself to us. What we see and the way in which we see, hear, touch or feel, is closely dependent on the structure and current state of the retina, diaphragm or whatever. Indeed it is plausible to speculate along the following lines. If we were so to alter our retinae that they became sensitive to electrons in the way that certain instruments are now sensitive to the latter, our resulting representations would not only be dramatically different from those which we have at present, but regarded as true pictures of reality they would be incompatible with them. And from this it follows, for reasons similar to those given earlier, that reality cannot itself possess the properties intrinsic to its representations. Once again we are forced to conclude that the intrinsic properties of our representations reflect not so much their cause as ourselves their recipients.

The relation between subject and object

A fourth and related argument for transcultural relativism turns on a more abstract consideration of awareness or apprehension. It is this. We usually think of apprehension as entailing some sort of relation between a subject and an object, between apprehender and apprehended. While this in general terms is acceptable, it is not acceptable to suppose that we can clearly separate out what is subject and what is object. The best that we can say of the subject *qua* subject is that it is that to which the object is presented, or represented. To attempt to say more is to give rise to the perplexities which confronted Hume, and which perhaps should have confronted Descartes before him. We can only know ourselves as knowers of objects, and the properties we ascribe to ourselves are drawn from, or at least are indissolubly related to, the objects of which we are aware. Equally, the best we can say of objects *qua* objects is that they are things apprehended by subjects. To grasp more clearly what it is for a thing to be an object is beyond us.

If for these reasons it makes no sense to try sharply to separate subject from object and object in turn from subject, for the very same reasons it will make no sense to say that such and such are the true properties of reality; that is, the properties of objects while unapprehended. In other words, whatever attempt we make to describe reality absolutely is doomed from the start.

An a priori argument

The fifth and final argument for transcultural relativism is an *a priori* argument from the possibility of there being radically different ways of apprehending reality. This possibility may be brought out in the following way. While our forms of apprehension are perceptual and propositional in kind, there can be and could be no demonstration of their uniqueness. For such a demonstration could only pursue one of two paths. It could proceed from a purely internal assessment of our modes of apprehension, or it could attempt to compare the latter with supposed rivals, arguing that these are either unintelligible or out of the question on some other grounds.

A purely internal assessment can lead nowhere. For uniqueness operates as an *exclusive* concept. To show that something is unique is precisely to show that it has, or can have, no rivals. But *ex hypothesi* a purely internal assessment considers no alternatives. It is therefore in no position to rule them out.

The method of comparison fares no better. For while we may 'conceive that' there are *prima facie* rival forms of apprehension to be considered, we cannot 'conceive of' them: that is, we cannot have any notion of them other than that they are different from our own. The reason for this is obvious. If within our present mode of apprehension we could 'conceive of' others, these necessarily would not be *radically* different from ours, and therefore could not constitute alternatives in the required sense. It follows that there is no possibility of our forming a sufficiently clear conception of supposed rivals for us to be able after analysis to dismiss them. Further, even if we could conceive of alternatives with clarity enough to examine and subsequently reject them, we could never know if or when we had exhausted their set. Indeed the latter might be infinite. Once again then, a uniqueness demonstration eludes us.

This fifth argument for transcultural relativism has so far been negative, showing that we cannot rule out alternative forms of apprehension. But are there positive grounds for allowing them in?

There are two such grounds. First we can appeal to tradition. With not very many exceptions, non-philosophers and philosophers alike have been prepared to allow for the intelligibility of a purely spiritual, non-temporal and infinite God. But the very mention of such a being brings with it the notion of a kind of awareness or apprehension very different from our own: an awareness which is for example not dependent, not temporal, not partial, not indirect, not articulated. Thus, to deny the possibility of kinds of apprehension other than our own is at once to deny what tradition has almost universally conceded — the intelligibility of the existence of God or other spiritual beings. Second, we can appeal to a point which was made earlier, arguing as follows. The human brain together with its processes of thought and perception may accurately be viewed as a means by which one kind of organism has successfully adapted to its complex environment. But given this, it is not only intelligible but highly plausible to suppose that there could be, and may even now be, organisms which have developed totally different but still apprehensive adaptations to their environment. Widely different structures, in a word, may produce widely different and consequently rival representations of reality. It may be worth adding that if at times we are inclined to disbelieve this and to consider our representations to be necessarily unique, this is not surprising. For the only way we have of apprehending reality is the way we have in fact. By analogy, a race of beings possessing only one sense might be tempted to think that there could be no others.

Supposed consequences of transcultural relativism and objections to it

The above arguments, while forming a sketch of what would require a book to elaborate, may at least serve to show that the claims recently repeated in educational circles that knowledge is not absolute, not 'out there', are not foolish claims. For they are, or at any rate can be, precisely expressions of transcultural relativism. However, many will continue to object to this latter doctrine on the grounds that they consider it internally unsatisfactory or because they think that it leads to educationally disastrous consequences. They believe, for example, that it leads to such claims as that 'anything goes'; that there is no such thing as truth; that even if there were such a thing as truth, we would have no rational means of attaining it; that one belief is as good as another; that what we call truth is a matter of individual or collective choice rather than of reality; that majority opinion is the sole criterion for what should count as true.

These objections need now to be looked at more closely, not only because no supposed weaknesses of a major theory should go unnoticed, but because in the present climate of educational dispute it is important not to confuse issues by attacking the wrong position. It is important to grasp that it is not the relativism of certain educationists which is at fault, but their views on the nature of that relativism and the consequences which they and some of their opponents think are contained in it.

Objections to transcultural relativism on the grounds of consequences

The simplest way to proceed from now on will be to set out the principal objections to transcultural relativism and at the same time briefly to show

133

how they can be met. A start will be made in this section with those objections which concern supposed consequences.

Objection 1. Transcultural relativism is generous to the point of absurdity. If followed through it allows for any proposition to be asserted and subsequently defended, on the grounds that it is true relative to at least one set of believers, actual or possible. In short, transcultural relativism endorses the view that 'anything goes'.

Comment. This objection is unsatisfactory for at least two reasons. First, the transcultural relativist is not a subjective idealist, and therefore does not deny that there is a reality independent of us and responsible for the representations we have at any given moment. In other words, the transcultural relativist is not constrained to believe any more than the rest of us that if the cat is on the mat this is a question of choice rather than reality. Nor is he constrained to believe that the *manner* in which men apprehend and make sense of reality is a matter of choice. On the contrary, he will assert that when we apprehend reality, we *can* do so only by perceiving, conceptualising, propositionalising and reasoning. Neither the existence of facts nor the manner of their presenting themselves is at our pleasure. Not anything goes, therefore, but only what is supported by perception, conception, reason and reality.

Objection 2. Even if transcultural relativism is absolved from the accusations contained in the last objection, it is not to be absolved from the kindred allegation that it destroys the notions of truth and falsity. For, whatever else the doctrine holds to, it is at least committed to the view that *in the final analysis* no proposition may be taken to be true.

Comment. The transcultural relativist does not in this way destroy the notions of truth and falsity, nor even blur the distinction between them. For again, if the cat is on the mat, the sorts of reasons that the relativist has for saying so are as good as his opponent's, and they are as good as the latter's precisely because they are the same. Both can call on such things and only such things as the evidence of the senses, the testimony of witnesses and the cat's past behaviour.

What no doubt gives rise to the present kind of objection is the recurring feeling that since according to the relativist propositions do not disclose the nature of reality as it is in itself, they therefore cannot be true. However, this is to misunderstand the relativist. His doctrine is a doctrine *about* true propositions, not a doctrine to deny their existence. To claim that it is is merely to show allegiance to the contrary belief about true propositions: the belief that their status is absolute. It is to demonstrate nothing.

(If it be urged on grounds of analyticity that the notion of truth already contains a commitment to its being considered absolute, it is open to the relativist to abandon the notion altogether and to speak instead of 'warranted beliefs' or something of the sort.)

Objection 3. Every type of relativist is ultimately driven to define truth in terms of majority opinion; for given that propositions have no absolute status, he has no other way of accounting for the differences between those which are true and those which are false. However, such a definition quickly leads to absurd consequences. Confronted with a proposition concerning which there is as yet no majority opinion, each individual will be forced to wait and see what the majority will believe; but the majority will not be able to form a belief until the individuals constituting it have first made up their minds. Inevitably then there will be a deadlock.

Comment. The relativist is no more concerned and no more required to define truth than the non-relativist. His purpose rather is to uncover and bring to light one important aspect of true propositions: that they do not reveal reality as it is in itself. To the question of how he is to decide which propositions are true and which are false, the answer is that he must decide in the same way as everyone else. That is, he must look to the evidence of his senses, to the evidence of the past, to the community's best established beliefs and theories, to its basic epistemic principles. In a word, like the non-relativist he must behave rationally.

It might be worth adding, since there is some confusion on the point, that the relativist is not debarred from any particular theory of truth, not even from the correspondence theory. For there is nothing to prevent his asserting that a proposition is true if and only if it corresponds to reality *as the latter is represented to us*. For this reason, the proposition, 'Snow is white', is true for the relativist as for the rest of us, if and only if snow is white.

Objections concerning supposed internal weaknesses of the doctrine

To turn now from objections concerned with supposed consequences of the doctrine of transcultural relativism to those concerned with the doctrine itself or with its foundations.

Objection 4. On two separate scores the doctrine of transcultural relativism is self-refuting. First, if taken seriously it itself is relative. But surely those who espouse it cannot mean it to apply to itself and thus to lie open to rejection on the grounds that it is merely one view among many. Second, the doctrine is self-refuting for this reason, that if it is true it is consequently not more true than false. For if it is true, on its own showing it is true to one set of believers or apprehenders and may well be false to another.

Comment. First, the transcultural relativist should have no qualms about considering his doctrine itself to be relative. Second, he is not committed to seeing it as no more true than false. The reason for both of these claims is that he is compelled by *argument* to say that none of our forms of apprehension are able to grasp reality as it is in itself. From this he is led further to conclude that, given the possibility of other kinds of apprehension, our own kind together with its beliefs *and* doctrines is relative. On the other hand, while he asserts that radically different kinds of apprehension are possible, he is under

135

no compulsion to grant that, within what constitutes *our* kind, transcultural relativism may be treated as equally true or false. On the contrary, his claim is that all reason and argument compel the acceptance of its truth.

Objection 5.   The transcultural relativist presupposes what he claims to deny. For he presupposes that men exist with their bodies, brains and organs of sense, and then goes on to argue that in reality these things do not exist at all. In this way, therefore, he denies in his conclusion what he asserts however covertly in his premises.

Comment.   There is a confusion here similar to that in the second objection. The transcultural relativist does not in his conclusion deny what he asserts in his premises, since the latter concern only the philosophically neutral world which he takes as his point of departure: the world in which such things as hands are as acceptable to a Berkeley as they are to a Moore. The focus of disagreement then between the relativist and his adversary is not whether there exist such things as hands or brains, but whether these latter items as they are perceived and conceived of form part of reality as it is in itself. The relativist concludes that they do not; but what he concludes is an analysis, not a denial of what earlier he asserted.

Objection 6.   The doctrine of transcultural relativism is counter-intuitive, since the truth of at least some propositions appears obviously to be absolute. Examples of these are the following. At least something exists. There are such things as beliefs. Propositions cannot at the same time be true and false.

Comment.   This objection overlooks the philosophical rule that when intuition is found to be at odds with argument, the latter should prevail. But many arguments have by now been advanced for the view that no propositions reveal reality as it is in itself, and this of course includes such propositions as those referred to. Their truth, then, cannot be absolute.

Further, there is an obvious explanation of why the propositions referred to appear to be absolute. It is that the representations through which we apprehend reality in fact comprise *inter alia* beliefs, propositions and concepts like 'something' and 'existence'. Because of this, it is incorrigibly true that within that set of representations there are beliefs, that these cannot simultaneously be true and false, and that something may properly be said to exist. But that these propositions are incorrigibly true should not be confused with their being absolute. For while there are beliefs it is of course incorrigibly true that there are beliefs; but this does not entail that while there are beliefs all or some of these disclose reality as it is in itself.

Objection 7.   The conclusions of transcultural relativism are too paradoxical to be credible. If pressed they amount to the scarcely intelligible claim that there is a certain something, existing in a causal relation with another (or the same) something, as a result of which there are sets of representations through which the first something is apprehended or brought to the awareness of a further (or the same) something.

Comment.   That the conclusions of transcultural relativism are paradoxical is not sufficient reason for dismissing it as unintelligible or beyond credibility. In any case there is nothing unfamiliar in our having to refer to a thing whose only properties known to us are relational, and of which we know nothing beyond its effects. 'Genes' were perhaps like this for a long time; so was (and is) the 'unconscious ego'; so are, it would seem, what we refer to in general terms as 'the ultimate constituents of physical reality'. The paradoxicality of transcultural relativism, then, lies not in its kind of utterance but in the universality of its scope and application.

Objection 8. The doctrine of the transcultural relativist cannot properly be stated, since he attempts to speak of reality in a language which on his own admission can apply only to representations.

Comment. The transcultural relativist is not a positivist. He does not admit that language has application only to our representations, only to items of immediate acquaintance. Nor is there any good reason why he should. As was said in the context of the last objection, there are many uses of language which stretch our concepts beyond the range of immediate experience. We are all familiar with talk of infinities, α-particles, photons, electrons, quarks and the like; and we should see the relativist's talk as being of the same kind.

Objection 9. Beliefs about our representations if true are true absolutely. For if they do not reveal the nature of reality as it is in itself, they do at least reveal the nature of our representations as *these* are in themselves; and in that sense they are absolute.

Comment. The relativist is not forced to any such conclusion. For given that all beliefs are representations, it follows that even beliefs about representations are themselves representations. They cannot, therefore, be held directly to disclose what they are about, and consequently cannot in any sense be held to be absolute.

Objection 10. The case for transcultural relativism leans much too heavily on the claim that the best account of things available to us is the one which embraces the findings and theories of science. Not all philosophers will accord the latter pre-eminent status. On the contrary, many of them will say that if the findings of science threaten our belief in such things as our own two hands or proper selves, so much the worse for the findings of science.

Comment. This objection and others of its kind can scarcely be met in a sentence or two; they may even constitute a permanent focus of philosophical debate. Nonetheless two short comments may be made in favour of the relativist here. The first is that he offers a systematic, well-articulated and all-embracing account of things, including therefore hands and selves. The second is that he may justly point out that the agreement of scientists concerning most things in the physical world is considerably more impressive than that of metaphysicians on the status of hands and selves. It is this, he will claim, which warrants his confidence.

The conclusion to this chapter then is that knowledge is not absolute, not something transculturally 'out there'. But those educationists who hope to make something of this are to be disappointed, just as those who fear that something will be made of it are to be comforted.

FURTHER READING

*Acton, H.B. "Idealism", *Encyclopedia of Philosophy*, Edwards, P. (ed.) New York, 1967, vol. 4.

Ewing, A.C. *Idealism. A Critical Survey*, London, 1934.

*Hocking, W.E. *Types of Philosophy*, Type 5, "Idealism", 3rd. ed., New York, 1959.

*Schopenhauer, A. *Essays and Aphorisms*, Hollingdale, R.J. (tr.),London, 1970, especially the Introduction by Hollingdale and the third essay, pp. 55ff.

Schopenhauer, A. *The Fourfold Root of the Principle of Sufficient Reason*, Payne, E. (tr.), La Salle, Ill., 1974.

*Taylor, A.E. *Elements of Metaphysics*, London, 1903, bk. 2.

N.B. More advanced readings are: Kant's *Critique of Pure Reason,* Schopenhauer's *The World as Will and Idea,* Nietzsche's *The Will to Power.*

FOOTNOTES

Introduction

1. Brief but useful discussions on this point will be found in Lawton (1975), pp. 28ff. and Cooper (1980), pp. 133ff. My own definition will be given in Chapter 1.
2. The German phenomenologist Husserl and others gave their own sense to the words 'world' and 'reality', and this carried through into works like Berger and Luckmann's (1971) *The Social Construction of Reality*.
3. Many papers in Young's (1971) (ed.) *Knowledge and Control* are poorly written and in parts impenetrable. Young's 'explanations' in his dialogue with John White are no better (see White and Young (1975)), and even his most sympathetic commentators struggle to make sense of what he has to say (see Clark and Freeman (1979) and Freeman and Jones (1980)).
4. It is difficult to find systematically argued expositions of the case for cultural relativism, and one of the difficulties I face in this book is having to construct arguments as well as criticise them. Cultural relativism is widely accepted but rarely articulated.
5. Gorbutt (1972), p. 7.
6. Young (1971), pp. 5f.
7. Young (1971), p. 131.
8. Harris (1979), p. 74.
9. Harris (1979), p. 73.
10. Bloor (1976), p. 8 and *passim*.
11. Berger and Luckmann warn us that they use 'knowledge' and 'reality' in ways different from philosophers, but later in the book they (appear to) argue as if they were attempting to establish a radical philosophical thesis. I have asked many sociologists of my acquaintance what the book means to establish and have had almost as many different answers.
12. See, for example, Remmling (1973), pp. 9f.
13. See especially the early parts of the *Investigations* where Wittgenstein is criticising logical atomism, and *Lectures and Conversations on Aesthetics, Psychology and Religious Beliefs*.
14. See Winch (1958, 1967) and Phillips (1969, 1970). Winch of course claims that his doctrines are not radically relativist (see Winch (1967), pp. 38ff.).
15. See, for example, Quine (1953).
16. See Körner (1969, 1970).
17. See, for example, Ayer (1946), Strawson (1952), Wright Mills (1939).
18. See Kuhn (1962), Lakatos (1970, 1976), Feyerabend (1975).
19. Cooper (1980).

20. Cooper (1980), pp. 115ff., gives a special sense to 'pragmatist'.
21. Cooper (1980), pp. 112ff. There are several other, though mostly briefer, attempts to come to grips with the doctrines of Young and his colleagues: see, for example, Gorbutt (1972); Lawton (1975), pp. 56ff.; Flew (1976), pp. 9ff.; Pring (1976), pp. 67ff.; Bernbaum (1977), *passim*; Warnock (1977), pp. 106ff.; Sarup (1978), pt 1; Clark and Freeman (1979); Freeman and Jones (1980).

Chapter 1

1. To avoid confusion later it may be useful if I point out that by 'making no sense' here I mean 'making no sense to men in general'. Thus the onus is on the relativist to prove that this or that belief is such that it makes no sense to men in general to say that it is true (or false) to the exclusion of its rivals.
2. This chapter's arguments in favour of total cultural relativism are based on arguments to be found in Körner (1969, 1970, 1973). But this does not mean of course that Körner would accept my formulations and adaptations.
3. The general line of argument that I pursue against total cultural relativism has similarities with the line taken by a number of philosophers: see, for example, Mitchell (1962), Chaps. 6 & 7; Lukes (1970, 1973, 1974); Hollis (1970a, 1970b, 1972). But it has its roots in Aristotle's ideas on human nature and in Kant's transcendental deductions.

Chapter 2

1. It can be argued, for example, that the weight of observational evidence was against Copernicus. Stones fall to the foot of a tower; bodies do not fly off from the earth; the stars give no evidence of parallax (to the naked vision, which was all Copernicus and his contemporaries had); Mars and Venus do not appear to change in size (again to the naked vision). Copernicus persevered with his theory largely because it could explain retrograde motion without appealing to epicycles. Observational evidence in favour of it came later, with the use of telescopes and so on. For a good summary of the issue, see Chalmers (1976), pp. 64-71.
2. See, for example, Gregory (1966), Chaps. 1, 10-12; Chalmers (1976), Chap. 3; Pratt (1978), Chap. 6.
3. Scientists were wrong in their beliefs on spontaneous generation, for example, or on the inheritance of (most?) acquired characteristics. For some interesting comments on the first, see Lovell (1980), pp. 60ff.
4. Biologists, for example, see all sorts of things under the microscope as three-dimensional organisms, which the rest of us make no sense of at all. And the man in the street sees all sorts of things as *functional* items (books, cups, traffic lights) which 'in themselves' are lumps of clay, masses of iron and glass, and so on. See Chalmers (1976), pp. 21-25.
5. For example, scientists did not need many successes in firing rockets into outer space before they quite properly generalised about the behaviour of rockets, or *mutatis mutandis* many successes in constructing and operating nuclear reactors.
6. The various theories of inertia, for example, would have been disallowed, and so for that matter would most of physics (talk of mass, force, time, electrons, quarks and the rest).
7. For example, Newton's theories had wider explanatory and predictive powers

than those of his predecessors. More recently the interpretation of the red-shift as evidence of an expanding universe fits neatly into more general theories concerning light and the spectrum.

8. See footnote 1.
9. Thus Einstein 'rejected' the a-causal accounts in quantum theory. At the other end of the scale, Newton's theory was persevered with in spite of the conflicting evidence relating to the perihelion of Mercury.
10. Thus, for example, the supposed evidence concerning the orbit of Uranus turned out not to falsify Newton's theory: the presence of Neptune had not been discovered.
11. For example, on the question of parallax or the size of Venus it was wrongly assumed that the method of observation (naked vision) was adequate.
12. See footnote 2.
13. As an example illustrating the first point, commonsense evidence for a long time justified the belief that a continuously acting force was required to sustain motion. The same observational occurrences are now taken to support the opposite belief. As an example illustrating the second point, Darwin's theory survived Kelvin's thermodynamics.

Chapter 3

1. See for example Hull (1943), p. 400, or Merton (1967), p. 47.
2. For these views see the appendix to this chapter.
3. A quite brilliant survey of these various schools is to be found in Bernstein (1979). He refers to 'Empirical Theory' to cover a view very much wider than genuine positivism, but not wider than what some sociologists seem to have in mind when they speak of positivism.
4. The most obvious example from many that spring to mind is Adorno, who — as far as one can gather — deliberately wrote unintelligibly, to make clear his break with the Establishment. See the section on Adorno in Kolakowski (1978), vol. 3, and the admission by Marcuse that even he does not understand many passages of Adorno's writings (Magee (1978), p. 73).
5. A claim made by Worsley (1977), p. 19.
6. Bernstein (1979), p. 26, argues that a Popperian pattern of conjecture and refutation does not occur in the social sciences — on the grounds that there is no rational consensus among social scientists that the proposed theories are genuine empirical theories refuted by further empirical enquiry and experiment. Since there are wrangles about the precise part that observation plays in Popper's view of refutation, there is no point here in disagreeing with Bernstein on his Popperian remarks. But given the wider view of the progress of science which I have argued for, it seems perfectly obvious that conjecture and refutation take place as much in the social sciences as in the natural. Marx, Freud and Keynes put forward bold conjectures which were in large measure plainly refuted — empirically refuted — even if many have re-adapted their theories and kept them as what Bernstein refers to as 'general orientations'.
7. This suggests that in the extreme he need have no observational backing for his claim. This is true, in the sense that he need have no observational backing to make his explanation *preferable to others*. He may have economy, simplicity or consonance with other theories to recommend him.

8. This last phrase may seem to beg many questions. It may be objected that behaviour suitable to a belief that twins are birds will vary according to the 'form of life' of the person examining the observed behaviour. I look at this Winchlike position in the Appendix.

9. Skinner, for example, is constantly wrestling with metaphysical problems and is centrally concerned with the consequences of rival metaphysical views in matters touching on the nature of man, his freedom and so on. There is no justification at all for saying that in concerning himself with such matters Skinner is going beyond the pale of the social sciences. As has been argued several times in this book, man's mind is *not* divided in the way that such an objection would suggest.

10. See Trigg (1973), pp. 6ff., and Collingwood (1938), pp. 7-9, especially footnote 1.

11. See Chapter 1, under *The comparative 'argument' in favour of total cultural relativism*.

12. See Winch (1958), p. 119 and p. 72.

13. For a sharp statement of this view, see Lessnoff (1974), pp. 83ff.

14. See Habermas (1971) and the discussion by Bernstein (1979), pp. 185ff.

Chapter 4

1. The notion of 'better' here can be elucidated, if need be, in terms of John's wanting one thing more than another. For example, if John wants to go out with his girlfriend, Mary, more than he wants to stay at home by himself, then other things being equal John has *a better reason* for going out with Mary than for staying at home.

2. I do not mean here that 'having a reason for pursuing x' is definitionally equivalent to 'having x as an aim', but that they are analytically tied — as was argued earlier on.

3. This is not to go back on what was said about John Smith as an individual. What is meant here is that wherever there is a group of men, lack of co-operation in general would be irrational; *not* that it would be irrational for John Smith to leave the co-operation to others if they ensured the sort of conduct which he judged to be to his advantage.

4. This point may appear to be less than fair, since it looks as if while other theories do not entail respect for each individual, my theory positively allows for oppression. But in fact my theory only allows for it in the sense that it is compatible with it, and my point here is that every theory that I know of is compatible with it. If an intuitionist claims that his intuitions tell him that oppression is wrong, this does not mean that his *moral theory* is incompatible with oppression. Obviously it is not, since another intuitionist might consistently hold that oppression is acceptable.

Chapter 5

1. Strictly speaking, prescriptivism as a theory about the linguistic status of moral utterances does not *entail* relativism. But historically it was mixed up with Stevensonian emotivism and like the latter was rightly taken at least to be unusually compatible with ethical relativism.

2. My list of principles here owes much to Gert (1966), Chaps. 5 and 6. But this does not mean to say that Gert would agree with my arguments on all points. It may be

worth my mentioning too that my general approach both in this and the last chapter has much in common not only with Gert but with Warnock (1971) and Mackie (1977).

3. It should be obvious that my principle of justice or impartiality here does not commit me to a principle of consideration for each and every individual. It requires simply *enough* impartiality to allow societies to function.

Chapter 6

1. A number of colleagues have objected to me that what I now go on to establish as typical curriculum-content is altogether too obvious. To this, however, I would like to make a number of comments. First, while the content may be obvious, what I am primarily concerned with in this chapter is to show what are the underlying principles that can be appealed to to justify it. Second, the virtue of my theory is precisely to show *why* the content turns out to be obvious (because it is pegged to our basic goals and aversions). Third, given some of the quite astonishing things that have been said recently by educationists about the curriculum it seems very necessary patiently to repeat the obvious.

2. This view which has its roots in Rousseau, if not earlier, can best be studied now in Wilson (1971) or, in more popular form, in Neill (1968).

3. Probably most educationists think of schools as in some measure a means of altering society as a whole. But what I have in mind here are those who think of schools as *primarily* political battlefields. This is the sort of view which I find in many sections of Young (1971) and in the whole of Harris (1979). Whether or not the writers concerned would agree and be pleased with this description I do not know.

4. See Hirst (1974). In this section I am sadly brief on a very important area of controversy. But my purpose is to distinguish my own view from the views of others rather than to criticise the latter.

5. See especially Barrow (1976).

WORKS REFERRED TO IN THE FOOTNOTES

Ayer, A.J. *Language, Truth and Logic*, 2nd ed., London, 1946.

Barrow, R. *Common Sense and the Curriculum*, London, 1976.

Berger, P. and Luckmann, T. *The Social Construction of Reality*, Harmondsworth, 1971.

Bernbaum, G. *Knowledge and Ideology in the Sociology of Education*, London, 1977.

Bernstein, R.J. *The Restructuring of Social and Political Theory*, London, 1979.

Bloor, D. *Knowledge and Social Imagery*, London, 1976.

Chalmers, A.F. *What is this thing called Science?*, Queensland, 1976.

Clark, J. and Freeman, H. "Michael Young's Sociology of Knowledge: Epistemological Sense, or Non-Sense?", *Journal of Further and Higher Education*, 3 (1979), pp. 3-17.

Collingwood, R. *The Principles of Art*, Oxford, 1938.

Cooper, D.E. *Illusions of Equality*, London, 1980.

Feyerabend, P.K. *Against Method: Outline of an Anarchistic Theory of Knowledge*, London, 1975.

Flew, A. *Sociology, Equality and Education*, London, 1976.

Freeman, H. and Jones, A. "Educational Research and Two Traditions of Epistemology", *Educational Philosophy and Theory*, 12 (1980), pp. 1-20.

Gert, B. *The Moral Rules*, New York, 1966.

Gorbutt, D. "The New Sociology of Education", *Education for Teaching*, 89 (1972), pp. 3-11.

Gregory, R.L. *Eye and Brain*, London, 1966.

Habermas, J. *Knowledge and Human Interests*, Boston, 1971.

Harris, K. *Education and Knowledge*, London, 1979.

Hirst, P.H. *Knowledge and the Curriculum*, London, 1974.

Hollis, M. "The Limits of Irrationality", reprinted in *Rationality*, B. Wilson (ed.), Oxford, 1970.

Hollis, M. "Reason and Ritual", reprinted in *Rationality*, B. Wilson (ed.), Oxford, 1970.

Hollis, M. "Witchcraft and Winchcraft", *Philosophy of the Social Sciences*, 2 (1972), pp. 89-103.

Hull, Clark L. *Principles of Behavior*, New York, 1943.

Kolakowski, L. *Main Currents of Marxism*, Oxford, 1978.

Körner, S. *What is Philosophy?*, London, 1969.

Körner, S. *Categorial Frameworks*, Oxford, 1970.

Körner, S. "Logic and Conceptual Change", *Conceptual Change*, G. Pearce and P. Maynard (eds.), Dordrecht, 1973.

Kuhn, T.S. *The Structure of Scientific Revolutions*, Chicago, 1962.

Lakatos, I. "Falsification and the Methodology of Scientific Research Programmes", in *Criticism and the Growth of Knowledge*, I. Lakatos and A. Musgrave (eds.), Cambridge, 1970.

Lakatos, I. *Proofs and Refutations: The Logic of Mathematical Discovery*, Cambridge, 1976.

Lawton, D. *Class, Culture and the Curriculum*, London, 1975.

Lessnoff, M. *The Structure of Social Science*, London, 1974.

Lovell, B. *In the Centre of Immensities*, London (Granada), 1980.

Lukes, S. "Some Problems about Rationality", reprinted in *Rationality*, B. Wilson (ed.), Oxford, 1970.

Lukes, S. "On the Social Determination of Truth", *Modes of Thought*, R. Finnegan and R. Horton (eds.), London, 1973.

Lukes, S. "Relativism: Cognitive and Moral", *The Aristotelian Society*, supp. vol. 48 (1974), pp. 165-189.

Mackie, J.L. *Ethics*, Harmondsworth, 1977.

Magee, B. *Men of Ideas*, London, 1978.

Merton, R.K. *On Theoretical Sociology*, New York, 1967.

Mitchell, D. *An Introduction to Logic*, London, 1962.

Neil, A.S. *Summerhill*, London, 1968.

Phillips, D.Z. and Mounce, H.O. *Moral Practices*, London, 1969.

Phillips, D.Z. *Philosophical Enquiry*, London, 1970.

Pratt, V. *The Philosophy of the Social Sciences*, London, 1978.

Pring, R. *Knowledge and Schooling*, London, 1976.

Quine, W.V. "Two Dogmas of Empiricism", *From a Logical Point of View*, Cambridge, Mass., 1953.

Remmling, G.W. *Towards the Sociology of Knowledge*, London, 1973.

Sarup, M. *Marxism and Education*, London, 1978.

Strawson, P. *Introduction to Logical Theory*, London, 1952.

Trigg, R. *Reason and Commitment*, Cambridge, 1973.

Warnock, G.J. *The Object of Morality*, London, 1971.

Warnock, M. *Schools of Thought*, London, 1977.

White, J. and Young, M. "A Dialogue between John White and Michael Young". *Education for Teaching*, 98 & 99 (1975 & 1976).

Wilson, P.S. *Interest and Discipline in Education*, London, 1971.

Winch, P. *The Idea of a Social Science*, London, 1958.

Winch, P. "Understanding a Primitive Society", *Religion and Understanding*, D.Z. Phillips (ed.), Oxford, 1967.

Wittgenstein, L. *Philosophical Investigations*, Oxford, 1958.

Wittgenstein, L. *Lectures and Conversations on Aesthetics, Psychology and Religious Belief*, Oxford, 1966.

Worsley, P. *Introducing Sociology*, Harmondsworth, 2nd ed., 1977.

Wright Mills, C. "Language, Logic and Culture", *American Sociological Review*, 4 (1939), pp. 670-680.

Young, M. (ed.) *Knowledge and Control*, London, 1971.

INDEX

147